TAKING
MORE BIRDS

TAKING MORE BIRDS

A Practical Guide to Greater
Success at Sporting Clays
and Wing Shooting

Dan Carlisle &
Dolph Adams

Illustrations by Robert DeVoe

LYONS & BURFORD, PUBLISHERS

Design by M.R.P.

Printed in the United States of America

10 9 8 7 6 5 4 3 2 1

LIBRARY OF CONGRESS CATALOGING-IN-PUBLICATION DATA

Carlisle, Dan.
 Taking more birds: a practical guide to greater success at sporting clays and wing shooting/by Dan Carlisle & Dolph Adams; illustrations by Robert DeVoe.
  p.   cm.
 Includes bibliographical references and index.
 ISBN 1-55821-231-0
 1. Trapshooting.   I. Adams. Dolph O.   II. Title.
GV1181.C37   1993
799.3' 19 — dc20   93-4298
                                                              CIP

CONTENTS

ACKNOWLEDGMENTS

We would like to thank a few of the many people who contributed to this book. The staff at Cane Creek Shooting Preserve, where most of this book was written, unflaggingly helped us on the course and off. Our secretaries prepared the manuscript superbly, and Rob DeVoe did a great job on the illustrations. Our colleagues and shooting friends (Gerald, Wes, Mark, and Matt) critically reviewed the manuscript. We thank the staff at Olin Winchester and at Decot Hi-Wyd for useful information and for reviewing portions of the manuscript. Skip Hoagland and the staff at *Sporting Clays* helped us to get started and published several articles abridged from the text. Many range owners, fellow shooters, guides, and students with whom we have interacted over the years honed our love of shotgun sports. Lastly, our shooting friends and partners over the years have made both hunting and sporting clays sources of deep pleasure to both of us on each occasion we have shot with them.

Introduction

Sporting clays has its origins deep in the roots of bird shooting in England and Scotland in the eighteenth and nineteenth centuries. The increasing popularity of game shooting eventually led, in the early part of the twentieth century, to the formation of shooting schools by some of the best London gunmakers in order to help their customers shoot better. These schools typically employed clay pigeons (which had been developed in America in the preceding century) but threw the targets in a variety of presentations designed to simulate classic British hunting shots. For example, a driven bird such as a pheasant was and remains a popular feature of such layouts. Over the years of this century and particularly since World War II, sporting clays has become enormously popular in England and on the continent. In the early 1980s, this sport came to America and has since become the fastest-growing shotgun sport in this country.

The reasons for the rising popularity of the sport are not hard to find. In its own right, sporting clays is an exciting shooting game, which, in the eyes of many, presents greater challenges than more static games such as trap and skeet. The similarities between clay and wing shooting rightly tempt many hunters to use sporting clays for improving their game and as a substitute for live birds, particularly since clays are readily available throughout the year. Lastly, it is a pleasant and gregarious sport. How can you beat spending a beautiful day walking around a handsome clay course with good companions and friends? The growing inability of most people in this country to enjoy shooting game birds, readily and inexpensively, will undoubtedly continue to fuel the growth of sporting clays.

Over the past decade, the sport of clays in America has evolved in several ways. First, the tools, styles, and methods have changed considerably. Techniques for shooting sporting clays have evolved rapidly, as more and more able shooters experiment with the many variables in the game in order to improve their scores. This book reflects our current views on useful methods as seen in 1993, but we are confident that methods will advance considerably over the next five years.

A second major evolution over the decade has been in the nature of the targets presented and of the clay courses. Perhaps due in part to the rising skills of shooters, course owners/designers have increasingly presented more and more difficult targets. As a result, the sport has grown away from its hunting origins to some extent. One sees more and more shots which do not resemble hunting shots. We are pleased, however, to note that that pendulum is now beginning to swing back toward the origins of the sport. As more and more wing shooters and hunters take up sporting clays, the demand for shots which simulate actual hunting shots and for a closer marriage of the two sports grows.

This book is intended to improve one's ability to shoot moving targets with an unmounted gun. Although there are many ways of taking a given target and of mounting/holding guns, we present here an integrated system which will be useful to a wide variety of shooters. This shooting system has been perfected by Dan Carlisle over twenty years of shooting experience, including fifteen years of shooting instruction, twenty years of shooting game birds, and ten years of shooting sporting clays.

This book should appeal to shooters at all levels: beginners who are just taking up sporting clays and/or wing shooting; sporting-clays or wing-shooting enthusiasts who would like to improve their game; and competitors who seek a few extra birds to give them tournament advantages. For each of these groups, we recommend that you read this book carefully and attempt to master each chapter in succession. Use of the exercises at the end of each chapter, while perhaps appearing sophomoric, will aid you in retaining and using this information. The key to developing and improving your game, though, lies in the field and on the clays course. You need to practice constantly what you have learned. More importantly, you need to analyze, constantly and critically, what you are doing. Set definite goals for improvement. Lastly, taking lessons from a qualified instructor is one of the fastest ways to master shooting with a low gun.

This book has been written with sporting clays definitely in mind. The information contained here, however, is extremely pertinent to either lowland or upland game shooting. The basic methods we advocate for looking at targets, holding the gun, mounting, and delivering are equally applicable to both types of hunting. Mastering these skills will surely improve your wing shooting. The last step in this process is the entirely satisfying one of setting up a special clay layout for a given type of game (e.g. quail) and practicing on this layout for several weeks before the season opens. By mastering the techniques presented here, you will be pleasantly surprised when the next hunting season for your favorite game bird comes around.

We take deep pleasure in clay shooting as well as in wing shooting and have spent many happy hours on clay courses and in the field. The joys of an autumn day, good friends, and a shotgun are not deniable. In each of us lies the desire to achieve whatever we undertake *at the best level of which we are capable*. We hope this book will encourage and guide you in achieving that goal. We also hope that you will not lose sight of the fact that wing shooting and sporting clays are meant to be fun. Self-fulfillment is not incompatible with good sportsmanship and fellowship and one does not need to become overly competitive to achieve success in this or any other sport.

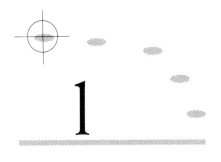

1

GETTING STARTED

To begin shooting well, one must know one's master eye and have a gun that fits (see Chapter 2). Don't neglect these two essentials; take care of them now. It's amazing how many people who have shot quite successfully for a long time do not know their master eye and do not have a good-fitting gun. In order to compensate, they have often acquired bad shooting habits that actually hold them back.

The *master eye* is the dominant eye — that is, the eye that controls our hand-eye movements. For example, when we pick up an object, our master eye determines the real location and the angle/distance from one's foot, so that one's hand reaches the object in one easy movement every time. This is well illustrated by the simple test for determining one's master eye. Look at a distant object with one eye closed; point to it. Open the other eye. Does the finger shift or not? If it does not, you have identified your master eye. To confirm this, try the experiment with the other eye. The object you have pointed to with the dominant eye closed should move away from the pointing finger when you open the master eye. It has been suggested that the speed of transmission of visual impulses is milliseconds faster from the dominant eye to the brain than from the non-dominant eye.

A more accurate way of determining the master eye is a card test. Take a square of cardboard or paper of about eight-inch size with a one-inch circle cut in the center. Hold the paper at about waist height. Focus, *with both eyes open*, on a distant object. With the cardboard at arms' length in front of you, keep the object in view while bringing the cardboard to your nose rapidly and instinctively so that the object remains in view. One eye is still looking through the hole. That's your master eye. If these tests are not conclusive, consult a qualified instructor.

I've determined my master eye — so what? If you have been shooting right-handed and have a dominant right eye or if you shoot left-handed and have a dominant left eye, proceed happily. If you do not, you now face a hard choice. We cannot recommend to any serious shooter a mismatch between handedness of shooting and master eye. Why can't you shoot right-handed if the left eye is dominant? Go back to the finger-pointing test. If you mount the gun beneath the non-dominant eye, you will hold the gun not on the target, but considerably to one side.

If you have a mismatch, you have two basic choices. You can switch gun shoulders (e.g., if you are left-eye dominant, you can begin shooting from your left shoulder) or you can patch your dominant eye (a small, opaque patch such as a piece of tape at the center of your eyeglass lens) so the gun shoulder you're accustomed to is now matched to an eye that is temporarily dominant. Don't try shooting with one eye; you lose too much important information. A variant of the second option is to use both eyes to pick up the target and then to close the dominant eye just before you actually complete the shot. We recommend changing shoulders. If you're taking up sporting clays seriously, now is a good time to change. While it may be harder at first, you will actually learn the game quicker than you would normally because you are learning all new methods without any previous bad habits. This choice will ultimately improve your bird shooting as well.

It is advisable to check one's master eye about every year.

People, as they age, can change relative dominance, so they run the risk of having a partially dominant eye.

Clothing

Four functional aspects of clothing merit comment. First, your clothing should be appropriate for climatic conditions. In summer, wear the minimum and, as the weather turns colder, add warmth by adding layers. Obviously, add water protection when needed. Second, wear clothing that is loose fitting, so your swing is not impeded in the least. On cold days, too many layers or too heavy a coat can make you feel like a little kid in a snowsuit who can barely move. Third, make sure your garments, particularly outer garments, do not interfere with gun mount. Although too many layers of clothing can interfere with mount in cold weather, we believe the biggest offenders in this regard are shooting vests, coats, and shirts that obstruct smooth mounting of the gun. Fourth, compensate in one way or another for the effect of your clothing upon stock length.

The number of accessories that one can potentially use and carry on a round of sporting clays or a day of wing shooting is long indeed. Most of these items can be quite useful in the appropriate circumstances, but they also represent additional weight to be carried throughout the day. Everyone has a different list of the minimum equipment necessary for them. Just remember: Your score will improve if you focus your attention on how the birds are flying and how other shooters are taking them rather than on fiddling with your accessories.

Exercises:

1. What is your master eye?
2. How did you test this?
3. If your handedness does not match your dominant eye, what have you done to correct the problem?

2

GUNS, CHOKES, AND SHELLS

Gun Selection

The shooter is faced with a wide variety of choices as to shotgun type. Here, we discuss some of the most fundamental choices to be made, as they pertain to sporting clays. We suggest you consult Bob Brister's book *Shotgunning, The Art and The Science* for a discussion on selecting guns for wing shooting. We are talking here about selecting a gun specifically for sporting clays. You can shoot clays with the field gun that you have now. Only when you decide that sporting clays is worth investing in another shotgun should you purchase a dedicated clays gun.

Sporting-clays guns typically have certain features. First, they have a slightly shorter stock and a smooth buttplate that curves slightly outward so the gun can be mounted easily. The buttplate must allow a smooth mount of the gun and must not hang up on your body or clothing. Second, the height of comb will typically provide the shooter with a flat sight picture down the rib so the gun shoots exactly where it is aimed. The stock is also designed to keep the head erect so the shooter has optimum visual control of the entire shooting field. An additional advantage of this feature is that straighter stocks reduce recoil. Many sporting-clays guns have a full-length, wide rib so it is easy to sight over. Lastly, sporting-clays guns typically have interchangeable chokes. Many new sporting-clays guns also have lengthened forcing cones, which improve patterning and reduce recoil.

Sporting clays is basically a twelve-gauge sport. An increasing number of tournaments present small-gauge events. Daily, we see excellent wing shooters do beautifully on a sporting-clays course with a small-gauge gun. Nevertheless, the inherent difficulties in sporting clays generally dictate the use of a twelve-gauge most of the time.

More difficult is the choice between an over-and-under or a semiautomatic. The semiautomatic offers the advantages of less weight, less recoil, and decreased muzzle jump. Together, these add up to more control. The over-and-under, by contrast, is the classic gun for sporting clays and offers certain aesthetic advantages. More practically, the over-and-under offers two barrels so that the shooter has the option of changing chokes between the first and second shots. Modifications discussed below can reduce recoil. In the end, the choice becomes one of personal preference. It may interest the reader to know that Dan Carlisle shoots a semiautomatic and Dolph Adams shoots an over-and-under.

We do not recommend either a side-by-side or a pump-action for sporting clays. The increased width of the side-by-side was designed originally for game driven toward the hunter, but these guns have the disadvantage, on many shots, of offering a greater visual obstacle between the shooter and the target. For example, a bird coming from beneath the shooter, where the shooter has to look around the barrel, will be more difficult to observe with a side-by-side. The time required to work the action on a pump makes it more difficult for the clay shooter to deal with true or following pairs. The pumping action also moves the barrel a great deal, which makes taking the second bird harder.

Sporting clays is a rapidly changing sport. When shooters first took up the game in this country, its origins in hunting suggested that shorter, lighter guns would be advantageous. In point of fact, this has not turned out to be the case. At present, we see most shooters using guns with barrels of at least twenty-eight-inch length. Interestingly, we see a strong movement among the best shooters toward even longer barrels; some even use thirty-two-inch barrels. The reason for this is as follows. Although a longer gun is more difficult for the beginning or intermediate shooter, its length makes it easier to swing through and establish lead for distant targets and thereby reduces the amount of gun travel needed to establish the longer leads necessary. For this reason, we suspect that over the coming ten years, sporting-clays guns will become somewhat longer than they are now. There is also a definite although perhaps less-pronounced trend toward heavier guns. Certainly most experienced shooters find that a five- or six-pound gun, ideal for wing shooting, simply moves too rapidly to be focused well on distant targets. Whether gun weights will continue to rise is not clear to us, but many shooters now use a gun weighing between seven and eight pounds.

The feel of a gun, as opposed to its fit, which is discussed below, is very important. The gun, like a golf club or tennis racket, must function as a natural extension of your hands. This is best achieved when the shotgun *feels* balanced when held in both hands. This is a very subjective point and varies from shooter to shooter for a particular gun. Said otherwise, different guns feel well balanced to different shooters. Although it is difficult to describe to you what we mean by a well-balanced gun, we all have had the experience of picking up a gun and exclaiming "Oh, what a sweet gun." Typically in our experience, this subjective feeling comes when the gun's weight is evenly distributed and one has the perception that the gun weighs less than it actually does.

The balance of a gun cannot be really determined until the gun fits appropriately (see below) for a number of reasons, including the fact that modifications to change fit usually add or take weight from various parts of the gun. A well-balanced gun can be mounted and controlled with a minimum of effort. A more objective way of assessing balance is to mount the gun instinctively under the eye of a good gunsmith, teacher, or shooter. Mounting an unbalanced gun will usually be accompanied by bobbing or weaving of the barrels; mounting a balanced gun should be achieved smoothly, easily, and with a minimum of effort. A gun can initially be estimated as balanced if its physical balance point rests somewhere between the two hands and, specifically, near the hinge pin of the barrel on an over-and-under. This is not, however, the end of the matter. Many strongly suggest that the greatest part of the overall weight should lie between the two hands.

A typical scenario is that a beginning clay shooter will trade guns every several months and go through as many as two to six guns in the first year or so of shooting clays. Why? One obvious explanation is, of course, that as our shooting skills and knowledge develop, we become more aware of differences between various guns as well as our own individual needs in a gun. We think the key point is that many shooters are not properly fitted at the start. Frequent trading of guns has two deleterious effects. First, it is expensive. Second, it does not allow the shooter to gain intimate familiarity with one gun.

We strongly believe that a shooter should get, as quickly as possible, one gun and then stick with it. First, the shooter has confidence in an old friend. Second, the shooter subconsciously becomes aware of all the nuances of gun fit and balance and can then rapidly, instinctively make the body adjustments necessary to make the gun work best for them. At many tournaments, we see superb shooters practice with new and very expensive guns but pull out their old friend of twenty or thirty years to shoot the tournament.

In the end, choosing among these variables in selecting a gun is, to a great extent, a matter of personal preference. The choice of a semiautomatic versus an over-and-under, of rib, of forearm, and of stock, particularly the hand grip on the stock, all depend on the individual.

Gun Fit

The three most important aspects of selecting a shotgun for sporting clays or wing shooting are gun fit, gun fit, and gun fit. How does one define a properly fitting gun? Formally defined, a properly fitting gun is one that, when mounted completely instinctively, will shoot where the shooter is looking—for those targets to be taken with that particular gun.

The most important piece of equipment for sporting clays or any other shotgun sport is a properly fitting gun. The make and cost of your gun are matters of taste and budget, but *your gun has to fit you well* if you are to shoot well. This is particularly true when you shoot a low gun and must mount rapidly.

What is a good fitting gun? First and foremost, the barrel, when instinctively mounted, must align with your dominant eye. The eye must look directly down *and* slightly above the sight plane of the barrel. It's an old cliche but still true. You don't have a rear sight on a shotgun; your dominant eye is your rear sight.

Second, the gun must fit comfortably and mount well. Perhaps the best way to begin assessing gun fit is by having a friend assist you. Be sure that the gun is completely unloaded: Double check this! Have your friend stand in front of you. Close your eyes. Mount the gun *instinctively* and bring it fully to your cheek. Open your eyes. Have your friend look down the barrel barely over the front sight at the pupil of your dominant eye. Your friend should determine whether the dominant eye is sighting down and slightly above the gun barrel or rib directly onto the front sight. If you have a middle bead on your gun, an additional check for you is to determine (after you've mounted in the instinctive fashion) whether the middle bead and the front bead are stacked to form a figure 8. These observations relate to *height of comb*. Next, is the barrel in line with the master eye? Specifically, is the line of sight directly aligned with the barrel? This observation relates to *cast of stock*. For these tests, you must make an instinctive mount with your eyes closed. Otherwise, you will adjust your mount to compensate for errors in gun fit.

Now ask if the gun fits your face. There are a number of reasons why a gunstock may not fit your face comfortably. Height, width, lateral position (cast) of the comb, and drop at the heel of the stock, in relation to the size and shape of your face and neck, are very important. For a majority of people, the standard shotgun sold in this country will fit reasonably well but you should check this point. Shape and width of the comb should roughly fit the face. For example, a person with wide cheekbones is likely to require either a cast-off stock (i.e., the stock bends away from the cheek) or a narrow comb. When the gun is well mounted, your head should be *fully erect* and not slumped over.

The third basic essential is proper stock length. Don't be misled by the old and incorrect saw that correct length of pull can be determined by matching length of the stock to length of your forearm. The length and build of your neck, the shape and contour of your face, and the size and contour of your chest and shoulders are all much more important in determining proper stock length. To determine whether your gun is of appropriate length, hold the forearm approximately in the middle, close your eyes, and mount the gun instinctively. Your head should be erect. The bridge of the cheek should rest firmly on the stock at about the mid-portion of the comb. More precisely, the thumb of your trigger hand should be one to two inches from your nose. The butt should fit naturally in the pocket of your shoulder. When you have adjusted the gun to this position, ask a friend to look closely at you and determine whether there is any space between the butt of fit in your gun and chest. If so, the gun is too short. Determine on the other hand whether the gun is resting too tightly on your chest or is difficult to mount. If so, the stock is likely too long. Bear your clothing in mind when establishing this point.

The last consideration in gun fit is to determine whether the gun mounts smoothly and easily from the low-gun position. A good-fitting gun, when the shooter is wearing a reasonable amount of clothing, glides smoothly into place into the shoulder pocket and onto the cheek without the need for any significant adjustment of head or shoulder. In this position, *the head should be erect* for best vision and the sight plane along the barrel should be clear. If these steps are followed, the gun should shoot where you are looking when you have mounted instinctively.

The most precise way of determining fit is to use a patterning board. This is described in the books by Jerry Meyer and by Steve Comus and Jack Lewis (See Bibliography). Summarized briefly, obtain access to a patterning board at a gun range. Treating the shotgun as a rifle, you should align both front and middle beads precisely on a marked point on the patterning board. Fire a round. Repeat this four times, so five rounds have been fired in all. Check the patterning board. The center of your shot pattern should coincide with the first marked shot on the board. If so, your gun, with that choke, is shooting where you aim it. Next, clear the pattern board and begin again. Look at the target spot and bring it into focus. Mount the gun and deliver the shot. Do this a total of five times. It is important that *each shot be delivered instinctively and rapidly*. If the resultant pattern centers on the marked spot, your gun, after mounting instinctively, is shooting where you are looking. By definition, it fits.

If your gun does not fit, we cannot recommend too strongly that you take whatever measures are necessary to make it fit correctly. The technicalities of an appropriately fitting stock are well described in Bruce Bowlen's *Orvis Wing-Shooting Handbook*. Remember that reasonably simple and inexpensive adjustments can be made to adjust fit. Height of comb can be easily raised by a pad. Length of stock can easily be increased or decreased by use of spacers and buttplate pads. A very useful device is the movable comb. These are inserted at the top of the comb on two metal posts, which can be moved from side to side. The comb can be moved from side to side, thus permitting the comb to be adjusted for either cast-on or cast-off. Height of the comb can be raised above or below the height of the gun stock by the number of spacers placed over the posts. This relatively inexpensive modification to a stock (one-hundred and fifty to two hundred dollars) along with an adjustable buttplate will take care of all but the most complex fitting problems. You may consult a good gunsmith who will need to work with you personally by using a try-stock to develop the precise measurements for a good-fitting stock.

We recommend that you fit your gun as soon as possible. Money invested in range fees and lessons, when shooting a gun that does not fit, is not well spent and keeps you from developing your shooting skills.

Let us now return to balance. Once you have a gun that truly fits well, make the extra effort necessary to insure that the gun is well balanced. If your gun is fitted to you, its balance has now become the major factor that will limit your ability. This is particularly important for those who shoot more than one gun. Very frequently, the subjective difference between various guns to a given shooter lies in whether each gun is balanced or not. Likely, the guns you prefer and shoot the best are those that are balanced. Complete the fitting process by adding or taking weight from the muzzle end or stock end until the gun is balanced.

Modifications

A large number of modifications can be made to reduce recoil. Lengthening the forcing cones will reduce recoil, but we note that more and more new sporting-clays guns are shipped from the factory with lengthened forcing cones. This is useful to consider if you are purchasing a new gun. We also recommend using a ported gun. The reduction in muzzle jump produced by porting will improve your ability to take the second bird in a pair in a more controlled and easier fashion. Porting by a professional firm is recommended, since ports that are too small or uneven can clog and ultimately discharge, causing injury. Lastly, recoil pads now on the market can be highly effective. For the shooter bothered by recoil, these are particularly useful.

We recommend exercising caution in gun modifications. Each of the modifications discussed here (after fit and balance) in its own right is useful but not necessary. To quote an old saying: "It's not the package, it's the address that counts." We have seen shooters become obsessed with this aspect of the game and spend endless hours and dollars worrying about modifications to their gun. These both could have been better spent on improving shooting skills. We firmly believe that for a fraction of the price spent on changing guns, the purchase of a good-fitting shotgun the first time or making the necessary adjustments (with the help of a good gunsmith) on your first shotgun will save you dollars and a great deal of time in mastering the sport.

Chokes

The fundamental principles of chokes and a great deal of information about them is contained in Bob Brister's *Shotgunning*. To summarize briefly, shot leaves the muzzle of a gun in a small, tight clump and then travels in an ever-expanding fashion. Chokes, which progressively constrict the barrel (Table 2.1), constrict the stream of shot as it emerges from the barrel. For any given choke, size of the pellet cluster (i.e., the pattern) widens and pattern density decreases as distance from the muzzle increases. Early in the shot's path, the stream is extremely dense but small. Later, it is

TABLE 2.1 Characteristics of Various Chokes

Name of Choke	Relative Constriction[1]	% shot Patterning[2]
Cylinder (Skeet1)	0 (5)	< 45
Improved Cylinder (Skeet) 2	10 (15)	45–55
Modified	20	55–65
Improved Modified	30	66–70
Full	40	70–80

1   Relative constriction in thousandths of an inch.
2   % of pellets patterning to a 30-inch circle at 40 yards.

very wide but can have many large gaps or holes. Between these two extremes lies an optimum range, where pattern size and pattern density come into reasonable balance. This optimum range increases as tightness of the choke increases. Thus, for each choke there is an optimum range. The optimum range depends on many variables including: 1) size (i.e., constriction) of the choke; 2) the actual choke or barrel employed; and 3) the shell, including shot size, powder, load, manufacturer, etc.

Shells

Shell selection is the subject of much debate and personal preference among shooters of all types because of the many variables involved. To simplify greatly, we first strongly recommend that the shells be of good quality and high consistency. Shells reloaded by the experienced shooter or quality target factory loads are necessary for delivery of a uniform pattern at a uniform speed. Consistency is perhaps even more important. In fact, we strongly believe that consistency is probably the biggest virtue in shells. Subtle differences in speed or patterning will affect your subconscious computer's ability to deliver hits. It is probably good to pick one type of shell, albeit purchased or reloaded, and stick with it.

In terms of shot size, one can use #7$\frac{1}{2}$ to #9 in sporting clays within association rules in this country. Again, consistency is a virtue. The arguments about type/amount of powder (and speed of shot) are endless. Again, your best friend is consistency so that your subconscious computer knows every time what to expect from a given load. Legally, one may employ no more than 3 or 3$\frac{1}{4}$ (NSCA/USSCA) dram equivalents of powder and 1$\frac{1}{8}$ ounces of shot. The choices in wing shooting are more complex and involve the game bird to be taken (see Bob Brister's book).

We urge using high-quality reloads or purchasing target loads, since there is a large variation in loads sold as dove/quail loads. In addition to the above, the hardness of the shot, the wad column, and the protection cup alter the performance of shells. In general, greater loads of powder, softer shot, removal of the protector cup, smaller shot, and wad columns with reduced cushioning properties all produce more open patterns. In contrast, smaller loads, harder shot, greater cushioning properties, larger shot, and addition of a protector cup all lead to a tighter column. These variables interact with the choke to determine the openness of pattern at a given distance. The effects of two of these variables (e.g., choke and shot size) on optimum range for lead shot are shown in Figure 2.1. Other factors such as the recoil sensitivity of a particular shooter may play a role in selecting shells. Jerry Meyer has an interesting discussion on these and other points in his book.

These variables, particularly load, shot size, and the type of powder, dictate the speed of the shot column. Together, these factors typically produce shot columns traveling in the range of 1050 FPS (feet per second) to 1200 FPS. This amount of variation will undoubtedly have small effects on the amount of lead required (see Chapter 8), given the length of a typical shot column (eight to

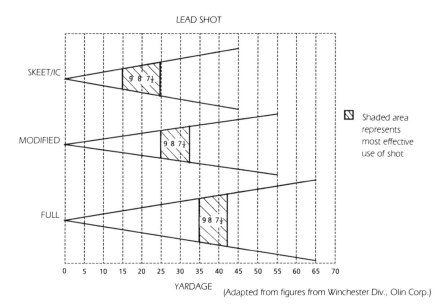

Figure 2.1 Relationship between choke, shot size, and distance on optimum pattern.

twelve feet) and the speed of most shot columns (1200 FPS). Again, we strongly recommend consistency.

Selection of shot size is a tradeoff. On the one hand, the larger the shot the more likelihood of breaking the clay with one pellet. On the other hand, the smaller the shot the more shot per load. Because some targets are particularly hard to break (e.g., standard targets on edge or rockets), we recommend using larger shot consistently.

To summarize an extremely complex subject without doing it justice, we recommend a $2\frac{3}{4}$- or 3-dram-equivalent load in a high-quality target load containing #7$\frac{1}{2}$ shot as an excellent all around shell for sporting clays.

Choke Selection

One can now put all of this information together. Choke selection begins with making an accurate estimation of distance (see Chapter 6). One can then begin to select the proper choke, remembering that the choke should work optimally at that range. The data in Table 2.2 present a general guide. Note, for example, the effect of shot size on optimum range.

The precise optimum range depends on many variables. We strongly recommend that you establish optimum range for each

TABLE 2.2 Optimum Ranges for Various Chokes[1]

Choke	Optimum Range in Yards[2]	Optimum Range in Yards[3]
Cylinder	15–25	24
Improved Cylinder	20–30	28
Modified	25–35	33
Improved Modified	30–40	37
Full	35–45	41

1   Data courtesy of Winchester Div., Olin. Corp.
2   Based on the data in Figure 2.2, using #7$\frac{1}{2}$ shot.
3   Based on use of 1$\frac{1}{4}$ oz of #6 shot with a 3$\frac{3}{4}$ dram equivalent load.

choke using one standard shell. Bear in mind that targets can be quite difficult to break. Every range is littered with unbroken targets penetrated by two to four pellets, particularly rabbits. We therefore recommend, as a general principle, a slight degree of overchoking. If the target is even more difficult to break (e.g. a target on edge), increase the degree of overchoking.

Let's take an example. A target at thirty-five yards could reasonably be taken with either a modified or an improved-modified choke (see Table 2.2). If the bird is on edge, we recommend use of no less than improved-modified choke. Remember: If you put the shot stream on the bird, it will break with a tighter choke because of the increased density of pattern. On the other hand, the shot stream from a more open choke can easily hit the target but not break it, due to decreased holes in the pattern. This becomes particularly true with increasing distance where the shot stream is rapidly losing speed and force. Some would argue that there is a tradeoff, in that better shooters would do better with tighter chokes, whereas less-accurate shooters would do better with more open chokes to give them a larger pattern. We do not believe this to be the case. We think that the advantages of a tight choke in density and accuracy of pattern outweigh the disadvantages for any shooter of using a looser choke.

The foregoing presents some useful general rules for selecting the appropriate choke. In actuality, optimum patterns depend on the gun, the actual choke used (i.e., the choke—not its designation) in that gun, and a precise shell (i.e., load, use, pellets, powder, etc.). We strongly recommend that you determine the optimum conditions for your gun, chokes, and shells at distances of from twenty to sixty yards.

Exercises

1. What steps have you taken to determine whether your gun fits you properly?

2. Is your shotgun balanced?

3. What steps have you taken to insure that the gun is balanced?

4. Give the optimum ranges for taking a target with a cylinder choke, an improved-cylinder choke, a modified choke, and a full choke.

5. What shells are you shooting at sporting clays?

6. Have you patterned your chokes?

3

BEGINNING TO LOOK AT TARGETS

Sporting clays is a difficult shooting sport. Although the clay targets themselves, their presentation, and their visibility vary widely, *bringing the targets into crisp focus at the right time is essential* to hitting them. The *true* speed, angle, and distance of a target may be hard to discern and can actually mislead the shooter. This chapter and the next will teach you how to integrate three key factors necessary for successful shooting: 1) *analyzing the true path of the target* and its presentation in order to set your body, hands, and eyes in the best position to carry out the subsequent steps; 2) *seeing the clay target clearly and bringing it into sharp focus* at the right time and place; and 3) *an active, vigorous method of moving the body, mounting the gun, and shooting the target* (Chapter 4). These basic skills also apply equally to wing shooting.

Analyzing the Target

The first step in breaking any target is to look at it carefully and analyze its path. What is the target really doing? Take every available opportunity to observe targets throughout their full path — from several angles. Most targets will tend to be a blur from the trap out to six to eight feet. After this point, watch the target carefully throughout its flight path. Some key questions are: How far out is it? Is it coming to you or going away? What is its angle? Is it rising or falling? When is it rising and when is it falling in its path? What is its speed? We'll talk about some optical illusions that make judging the real path of a target difficult in a later chapter (Chapter 6). For now, remember: You can be fooled by a number of factors. For example, if regular targets and minis are thrown from the same trap, the minis will appear to be more distant because they are smaller.

Next, determine where you wish to break the target — the *sweet spot*. This usually represents a window or a segment of the target's path. In some cases, the shooter cannot select the ideal sweet spot because obstructions lie between the shooter and parts of the target path or because the club has marked a designated shooting zone. Most of the time though, the shooter can choose freely where to take the target. If given this choice, select a point about halfway from the trap to disappearance of the target (Fig. 3.1). As the target emerges from the trap, it begins to lose speed. About halfway in its flight, it has slowed considerably but is typically still rising and still controlled by the power of the trap. *This is the sweet spot.* The target is slow but still controlled and therefore predictable in its flight pattern. After this, the target path is erratic and falling.

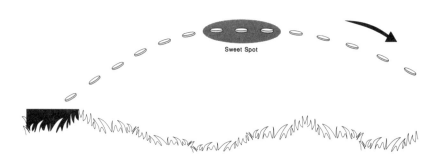

Figure 3.1 Flight path of a typical crossing target. Note that the sweet spot lies in the approximate center of the target's flight path.

Although this is a good general rule, there are obvious exceptions. For example, an incoming target may be out of control and even falling at thirty yards but it still may be of advantage to take the target at thirty yards rather than at sixty yards, where it is rising and under control. In sum, the shooter should predetermine for every stand the window or zone where the target can be best taken — well in advance of entering the stand.

Seeing the Target

Our marvelous visual system is extremely complex. Typically, we see objects first with our peripheral vision, which excels at picking up motion. The natural action of the eye is to bring a target or any moving object from the periphery to the central and most powerful part of the eye. This natural response leads to a concentrated focus on the object — lasting for just a fraction of a second. Try this. Point at an object across the room/yard and bring it into focus. You will be able to maintain the object in sharp focus for only a few tenths of a second. Your focus will then relax and you will begin to see things around the object selected.

When is a moving clay target in focus? The target will do two things when you achieve focus on it: 1) it will, for those few tenths of a second, appear larger, and 2) it will appear to be moving slower. Thus, a moving target in focus will appear briefly to be slower and larger; its size and speed will then revert to about what you saw before.

Focusing at the Sweet Spot

The body's visual and muscular systems are designed to bring *a moving object like a baseball into concentrated focus at the moment when our hands rise to grasp the ball.* The eyes guide the hands. This is an essential muscular skill for sporting clays. *You must bring the target into concentrated focus at the very moment when you make your shot.* This makes the target clearer and uses our instinctive hand-eye coordination to the fullest. In other words, *bring the target into focus at the sweet spot.*

How does one bring a target into focus at the sweet spot? Depending on the individual and the target speed, a reasonably predictable time lag occurs between when you begin focusing on the target and when it actually comes into concentrated focus. This lag time is essentially involuntary (not under the control of the shooter). Try this experiment. Look at a target moving about twenty yards away. Pick it up and begin focusing on it at a given point. Determine the point where it comes into concentrated focus, as determined by slowing and enlargement (Figure 3.2A). Repeat this by picking up the target ten to twenty feet later in its flight path. Again, determine the point at which the target comes into con-

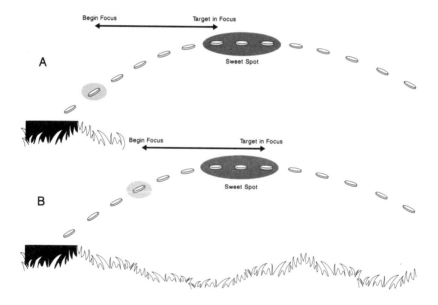

Figure 3.2 Bringing a target into focus at the sweet spot. In panel A, note that when one begins to focus early one brings the target into focus at an earlier point on its traverse. In panel B, we see that beginning to focus later brings the target into focus farther in the target's flight path. Since the time of bringing the target into focus is approximately the same in both situations, the distance the target will travel before it comes into focus will also be approximately same.

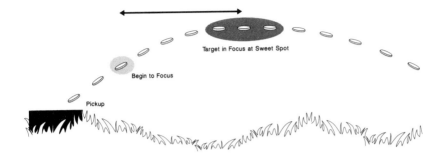

Figure 3.3 Bringing the target into focus at the sweet spot. By selecting the appropriate point for beginning to focus (not for picking up the visual blur of the target), one can bring the target into sharp focus at the center of the preselected sweet spot.

centrated focus. That will lie farther on the target path by about the distance between the second pickup point and the first (Figure 3. 2B). To match focus point and sweet spot, keep picking up targets at different points until the pickup point brings the target into concentrated focus at the sweet spot (Figure 3.3).

Exercises:

1. Have you learned on a clay course to define and determine the sweet spot for a wide variety of targets?
2. Have you practiced bringing a wide variety of targets into focus?

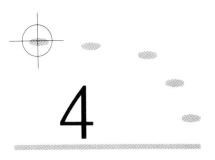

4

MOVE, MOUNT, AND SHOOT

John Bidwell's phrase "Move, mount, and shoot" aptly summarizes how to shoot with a low gun. We will now go into some detail on this process. Our goal is not to make shooting complex. Shooting with a low gun at rapid, variable targets is complex, and there's no mistake about that. We go into this amount of detail to break down and thus clarify the moves you must make during this *complex, integrated, and rapid sequence of motions* in order to hit targets consistently. For a while, you will be consciously putting all these muscular activities together. Soon, the movements will be become second nature and then unconscious. At that point, a highly complex process has turned into a natural, smooth, and instinctive set of motor skills that will make you hit targets easily.

Basics of Clay and Wing Shooting

Stance is the first important part of clay and wing shooting. It is literally the foundation on which your shooting is built. Stand so that your left shoulder (assuming you're right-handed) points to the sweet spot. Hold your feet reasonably close together (i.e., from twelve to fifteen inches to shoulder-width apart). For most shots, rest your weight about evenly on both legs but slightly more on the forward leg (i.e., sixty percent/forty percent); for overhead shots that require you to bend backward, distribute your weight forty percent/sixty percent. Bend both knees slightly. After the gun mount is complete, the body should pivot from the waist down. Your hands, forearms, arms, shoulders, chest, and head (when the mount is completed) should then lock into one unit (think of a mobile gun turret) which tracks the motion of the bird. This stance (forward knee pointing at the sweet spot) will allow you the maximum amount of body flexibility and gun movement through the sweet spot. Try this. Stand loosely in the shooting stance, holding the gun unmounted and parallel to the ground at roughly waist level. Swing the gun from side to side. Adjust your position until the amount of travel through the sweet spot is maximum. Actually, you will want more gun motion past the sweet spot than behind, because of lead. Now see where your shoulder points. For most people, it will point at the sweet spot or slightly in front of it. For others, where the left foot points will mark this spot.

Holding the gun correctly is also key. For the right-handed shooter, the left hand is your power hand. The left hand, working closely with the eye, can find the bird for you — if you let it. Place the forearm of the gun in the palm of your left hand. Extend your forefinger along the forearm, pointing toward the end of the barrel (Figure 4.1A). Pointing is the most accurate and natural way of identifying a moving object. Naturally and instinctively, your hands and eyes will coordinate. You can take advantage of this response by pointing your left hand, thus the gun, at a moving clay to improve hand-eye coordination. Grasp one side of the forearm with the thumb; use the other three fingers to grasp the other side. Hold the forearm relatively tightly. You don't want a death grip but you must be actively and vigorously in charge of the gun. Make sure the way you hold the forearm does not cant the barrel in either the unmounted or mounted position. Check this several times. The hand and arms should be relatively straight and not flexed or extended (forearm at a 45-degree bend in the elbow).

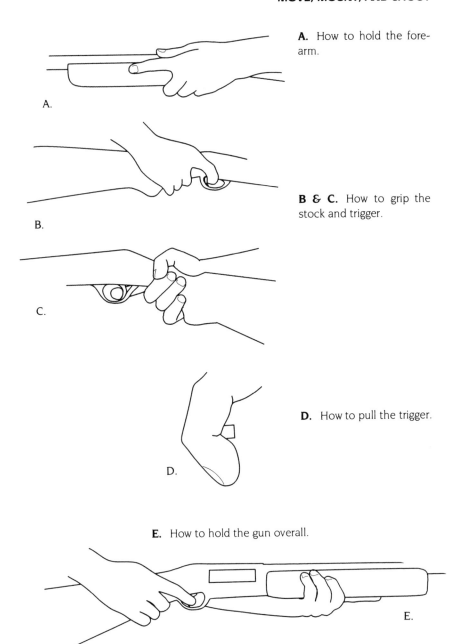

A. How to hold the fore-arm.

B & C. How to grip the stock and trigger.

D. How to pull the trigger.

E. How to hold the gun overall.

Figure 4.1 How to hold the gun.

The hand holding the stock, by contrast, is there mostly for support. The grip with this hand should also be relatively firm, but remember that power and action reside in the forearm hand. Place your hand on the stock so that the index finger comfortably comes around the trigger (Figures 4.1B and 4.1C) and so that the trigger is pulled by the flexion point of the first joint of the index finger (Figure 4.1D).

Sporting clays, almost by definition, is a low-gun game, as is wing shooting. Any clays tournament will require you to hold the gun below a certain point. There are two basic rules for determining this point: 1) the top of the gun must be visible below the armpit; or 2) the top of the gun must be held below the nipple line. It is easier to learn to hold the gun always in one legal position (the latter), and thus avoid having two different mounts. The rules do not call for you to hold the gun beneath the armpit; that is, the height

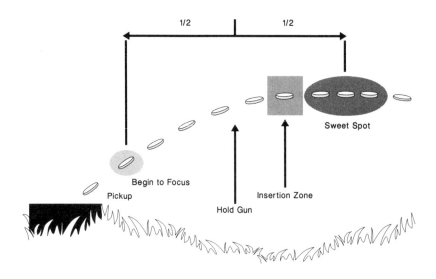

Figure 4.2 Where to hold the gun. Hold the gun barrel approximately one-half of the distance between the point where you will begin to focus on the target and the center of the sweet spot. Note that you will move the barrel of the gun smoothly in a rising arc into the flight path of the bird. The point where these two intersect is the *insertion zone*.

of the gun must be appropriate but you can hold the gun at the front edge of the body.

Where should you hold the barrel? Remember: The *least gun motion leads to the best results*. Therefore, hold the barrel of the gun on the line of flight of the target. If the target is a high target, hold the barrel high. If it's crossing, hold the barrel in front of you. If the target is below you, hold the gun barrel down. An easy way to establish this line is to pretend that an imaginary string runs between your nose and the flight path of the clay. This is approximately the height at which to hold the barrel. To be precise, hold it slightly below this string. If you hold the gun exactly on the path of the clay, you will block vision of the bird at some point. Hold the gun laterally about halfway between the focus spot and the sweet spot (Figure 4.2). Do not cant the barrel.

Put all this together with what you have already learned and mount the gun. Stand with your shoulder pointing approximately toward the sweet spot or where you plan to take the bird. Put about sixty percent of the weight on the front foot. Hold the gun so

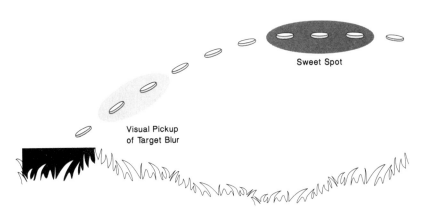

Figure 4.3 Pick up of target. Pick up the target approximately six to eight feet out of the trap when it is still a blurred visual image. After first pickup of target blur, you will subsequently reach the point where you begin to focus on the target in order to bring it into focus at the center of the sweet spot.

that the barrel is slightly beneath the flight path. Place the gun barrel at a point about halfway between the pickup spot and the sweet spot. Look back toward the trap—about six to eight feet out. Hold head erect.

Pick up the target when it enters your peripheral vision as a blur (Figure 4.3). Begin your mount. Actively point the left hand toward the path of the moving bird and bring the gun toward the insertion point. Think of the path of the gun as describing a gentle arc or parabola. In other words, bring the gun on a gently curving path to the flight line of the bird (Figure 4.4). Do not move the gun at a hard or right angle by mounting the gun onto the path and then beginning your swing. You have now brought the gun almost to the flight path of the bird. At the same time, you have been raising the stock of the gun toward your shoulder and begun swinging the gun. As the mount matures and at about this time, you will pass the begin-to-focus point; start bringing the bird into focus. Complete the mount by bringing the gun to your cheek and by rolling your shoulder slightly forward into the butt of the gun. You will find that this slight rolling motion is natural because the movement of extending your forearm toward the clay naturally brings your shoulder forward. You have now mounted the gun. At this point, you must be accurately looking down the barrel. Do not check this at this time; looking at the target and the gun at the same time will almost surely cause you to miss. Insert the gun on or behind the clay slightly before the clay reaches the sweet spot (Figure 4.4). During the mount, the eyes, head, hands, arms, and shoulders—in that order—will come into play to complete the mount. After that point, they should move as one unit. Once the mount is complete, sustain body and gun movement by swinging from below the waist in the order of hips, knees, and then ankles.

Be careful that your master eye aligns with the barrel. This happens more naturally on a left-to-right bird for a right-handed shooter. Here, the shooter readily looks back to the target with an erect and straight head. On a right-to-left bird, the right-handed

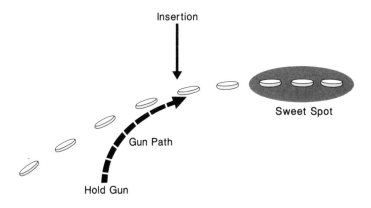

Path of Gun (Enlarged)

Figure 4.4 Insertion of the gun into the target path. Note that the barrel of the gun moves in a curving arc that gently intersects and merges into the basic flight pattern of the bird — much like the entry lane on a freeway. One of the key skills is to make this motion a gentle arc. Do not move the gun barrel at a right angle by bringing it directly to the path of the bird and then tracking the bird. Note that the merge spot is in the predetermined insertion zone.

shooter will tend, as he looks back at the target, to cant his head to the right. As he mounts, he will also tend to mount too soon (i.e., to the left of his true line of sight) and thus shoot in front of the bird.

Next, deliver the shot. There are a number of methods for determining when to pull the trigger or how much lead to put on the bird. We believe one's natural instinct is to pull the trigger when one pulls through the target so the target is crossed by the gun barrel and when you bring the target into focus. One can regulate lead by speeding up gun movement more or less, but this is hard to gauge and leads to lessened gun control. One can also regulate lead by varying the point at which you insert the gun into the flight path. We recommend this because it improves target visualization and gun control, and uses our natural instincts best.

Lead

When you insert your gun barrel into the path of a target and move through the target at a speed faster than the target, your barrel will cross through the bird. At the same time, your eyes should bring the target into focus. The point of delivery will naturally lie after the barrel crosses the bird and when the eyes have brought the target into focus. At that moment, your natural instinct is to pull the trigger. This is the key. *Your natural tendency is to coordinate hands and eyes in such a way that you bring the gun and the target together and focus the eyes on the target at the same time.*

Let's take a target that is moving rapidly. Just before the sweet spot and in the insertion zone, insert the gun on the target path very close to the rear of the target; you should complete the mount

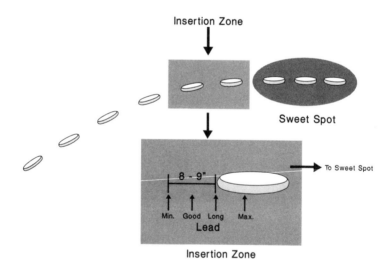

Figure 4.5 Lead on close and intermediate birds. For birds where the lead is that of a thirty-yard crosser or less, insert the gun barrel on or behind the target. The insertion zone lies just behind the sweet spot. Mount approximately nine inches behind the bird for minimum lead, just behind the bird or on its tail for a long lead, and at the very leading edge of the clay for maximum lead. Move the gun in parallel with the bird and speed up slightly. When the barrel crosses completely through the bird and when you have brought the target into focus, you will deliver instinctively.

at this moment (Figure 4.4). Move the gun only slightly faster than the target (i.e., one mph) by adding movement below the waist. After you have pulled the barrel through the target, a small fraction of a second will pass before your eyes focus on the bird. In that time, your gun will have traveled considerably beyond the bird—even though the barrel moves only slightly faster than the target. You will therefore deliver well past the target (or give the bird a relatively long lead). If you insert well behind the target (let's say eight inches) and again move the barrel only slightly faster than the bird, the lag time between pull-through and coming to focus will be much shorter (Figure 4.5). This will give a much shorter lead. There are several advantages to inserting close to the bird: Gun movement is minimal, gun control is maximum, and reading the target is easiest.

Let's pull all of this together and hit a clay (Figure 4.6). We've

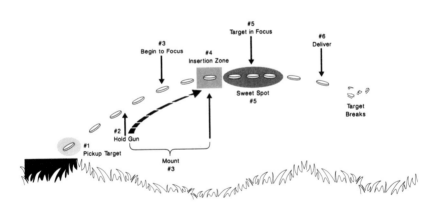

Figure 4.6 Key points along the flight path of the bird. # 1 — First pick up the visual blur of the target. You will hold the gun. #2 — At the first visual blur, you will begin moving the gun in a gentle arc during the mounting process (#3). During this period, you will also begin focusing on the bird (#3). When the gentle arc of the rising barrel intersects the path of the bird in the *insertion zone*, you will mount somewhere between nine inches behind the bird and the front edge of the bird. You will then speed up the gun slightly. You will bring the target into focus somewhere in the sweet spot (#5). You will then pull through at a speed slightly greater than that of the bird and deliver (#6). The target breaks!

TABLE 4.1

Point	Eyes	Head	Hands & Gun	Upper Body	Lower Body
Beginning Position (Fig. 4.7)	On Pickup Point	Turned Back to Trap	Gun in Hold Position	Shoulder Pointed to Sweet Spot	Shooting Stance
Pickup of Blurred Target (Fig 4.8)	Pickup Target Blur/Motion	Begin to Move with Target Flight	Actively Point to Path of Target and Push Gun Forward	Assitin in Pointing to Path of Target	Shooting Stance
Beginning of Mount (Fig. 4.9)	Moving with Target on Flight Path	Moving with Target on Flight Path	Begin Mount by Starting to Raise Stock	Begin Shoulder Movement for Mount and Begin to Swing Upper Body	Shooting Stane
Mature Mount (Fig. 4.10)	Begin Concentrated Focus on Target	Moves with Target on Flight Path	Mount Matures as Gun Barrel is Being Raised to Line of Flight and Gun Stock is Being Raised to Shoulder; Swing Gun with Target		Shooting Stance
Insertion of Gun (Fig 4.11)	Continue toward Focus	Moves with Target	Mount Completes and Gun is Inserted on Target		Begin to Move at Waist
Swing Through the Sweet Spot (Fig. 4.12)	Concentrated Focus on Target Achieved	Lock Together and Move as One — Continue Lock of Eyes, Head, Hands, and Upper Body	Continue Lock		Move Hips and Knees to Pull Through Target
Delivery		Continue Lock of Eyes, Head, Hands, and Upper Body	Pull Trigger		Coninue to Move to Follow Through After Delivery

talked about the pickup spot, the spot for beginning to focus, the spot for gun hold, the insertion zone, and the sweet spot/point of concentrated focus. When you get into the stand, make a judgment of necessary lead and determine whether you want to insert on the bird for longer lead or farther back for lesser lead. Now integrate these points on the target's flight path with definite parts of the mounting action. John Bidwell's phrase "move, mount, and shoot" is very telling. (1) *Visual pickup of the bird equals the moment pointing begins.* Also, begin to focus on the target then. (2) *The insertion point equals completion of the mount.* (3) *The sweet spot equals delivery (shoot).* The target breaks later.

You're ready now. Hold your head erect. Hold the gun about halfway between the pickup spot and the sweet spot (Figure 4.7). Pick up the blur of the target visually, begin to move your hands, and point at the target (Figure 4.8). Swing your arms with the bird as your mount matures and begin to focus on the clay (Figure 4.9). Complete the mount (Figure 4.10). The *gun should settle into the shoulder socket when the gun passes through the insertion zone* (Figure 4.11). Bring the stock to your cheek. Pull through the target *in the sweet zone at a speed slightly greater than the target* (Figure 4.12). Bring the bird into sharp focus. You will now instinctively pull the trigger and deliver!

For a right-handed shooter, a left-to-right bird may be easier. You can easily look back at the trap by swiveling your head and still keep it erect. On a left-to-right bird, it is easy to drop or angle your head when you turn back. It is also easy to mount too soon. These will cause a skewed, misaligned mount. The cure is obviously to hold the head erect and to put the stock to the cheek at the right time.

Remember two points. First, the entire mount should be a smooth, positive, active, and continuous movement of hands and body coordinated with the eye. Movement during mounting is with the upper body; movement after mounting is with the lower body. Second, this sequence allows you to take advantage of your body's natural tendency to bring hands and eyes into closest coordination.

Figure 4.7 Beginning position.

Figure 4.8 Pickup of blurred target.

Figure 4.9 Begin mount.

Figure 4.10 Mature mount.

Figure 4.11 Insertion of gun.   **Figure 4.12** Swing through sweet spot.

We've now given you some ways for roughly estimating where to look, where to hold the gun, where to insert, and where to take the bird. We will go into more detail on these matters in subsequent chapters. This basic scenario of inserting on or behind the bird is useful for all but the longest of leads. Typically, this would therefore cover leads on anything up to a crossing bird at thirty or more yards. With leads greater than this, a modification of our method will be described in a subsequent chapter (Chapter 8).

Remember for now, the details of these procedures not only can be varied, but *must be* varied by the successful shooter. When you step into the stand, set up the best combination that you can predetermine for taking that target. After you've made your first shot, ask yourself why you missed it or, if you hit it, where you were. You may need to make one or more adjustments in hold point, insertion point, or where you hold your head in order to break every target cleanly and completely. We will talk more about this art in later chapters, but it's a key for the highly successful shooter.

Your Subconscious Computer

The subconscious part of your mind (absolutely not the conscious) controls hand-eye movements and coordinates them precisely with moving objects in your environment. Your subconscious is essentially a built-in computer that will make, without your conscious awareness, small or large adjustments in elevation and forward allowance to deliver the shot pattern onto the target. We will explain later how to program and take best advantage of this computer. The computer is working all the time, can do amazing things, and can be programmed. You can make an enormous number of mistakes beginning with shooting with the wrong eye and using a poorly fitting gun, holding the gun down, mounting too early and poorly, and still break a target—all because your subconscious computer compensates for these mistakes. If you minimize the parts of your shooting style that burden your computer, you make it as easy as possible for your subconscious to deliver hits. Remember, too, the fewer mistakes you make in seeing the target, setting up, moving, and mounting, the easier it is for your computer to make the corrections necessary to hit tricky targets where instinct alone is not enough.

Exercises:

1. Describe the appropriate stance for clay or wing shooting. Where do your shoulders point in this stance?
2. Describe the appropriate method for holding the gun with right and left hands.
3. How do you determine where to hold the gun in relation to target path?

4. Draw a sketch map of the appropriate visual and hold points in a typical sporting clays shot. Integrate these with the three steps of move, mount, and shoot.

5. Have you played back enough shots from your subconscious computer so that you are confident you have gained the skill?

6. Draw a sketch of the insertion points for targets where you wish to achieve a minimum lead, a good lead, and a maximum lead.

7. What have you done to practice what you have learned about stance, gun hold, and gun mount (Hint: See Chapter 12)?

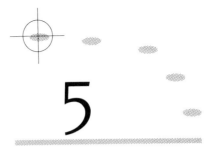

5

TARGETS AND THEIR FLIGHT

The flight of most targets follows a typical pattern: 1) rise; 2) plateau; and 3) fall (Figure 5.1). In the simplest case — targets thrown from a flat trap — the target will rise for one third of the flight path. It will continue on a flat plateau for one third of its path; it will then fall in the remaining one third. In the first portion of its flight, the target moves its fastest and generally rises. In the second portion, the target begins to slow down and travels flat but remains under the control of the trap. In the last portion of its flight, the target slows greatly, falls rapidly, and begins to wobble and travel unpredictably.

The distance and speed of a given target depend on at least four factors: 1) weight of the target; 2) angle of the trap; 3) length of the trap arm; and 4) tension/power of the trap spring. As a generalization, targets may travel from twenty to ninety yards horizontally or vertically. A typical travel path would be forty to sixty yards horizontally.

Speed of a target obviously depends on these same four variables. A typical target may emerge from the trap at sixty miles per hour (eighty-eight FPS) and slow very rapidly throughout the rest of its course. Contrast this with the typical speed of shotgun pellets — 1150 FPS to 1250 FPS.

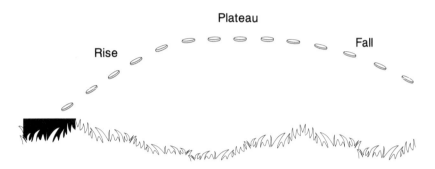

Figure 5.1 Typical flight pattern of a target.

Another factor in target path is variability of the trap. Depending on the particular trap, the skill of the trapper, and which arm of the trap is used, targets may vary vertically and horizontally from bird to bird. We suggest that maximum acceptable variation is five yards above or below the line of flight and five yards to or from the shooter.

In most cases, the number of targets *thrown at the same time* also determines flight path. Single targets, targets on report, and following pairs should follow approximately the same path. Not so for doubles, where the trap is loaded with twice the weight. As a result, doubles will usually fly slower and lower than their single counterparts. In the case of rising teal, the doubles will fly slower and reach a lower peak.

A last key variable is the type of target. At present, six target shapes and sizes are legal in this country: 1) the standard 110-mm domed target; 2) the 90-mm domed midi; 3) the 60-mm domed mini; 4) battues; 5) rabbits; and 6) rockets.

Domed targets, in each of the three sizes, have a high central dome and a ridged upper surface so that they resemble flying saucers. The standard targets have a dimpled top surface. These features give the standard target the most stable flying characteris-

46

tics of all the targets. The standard targets (110 mm) come in a variety of colors, including all orange, orange-domed, yellow-domed, all black, and all white. These targets tend to fly in a straight line from the trap, upward and outward, until gravity begins to take over and the target starts to fall and wobble. Midis, 90 mm in diameter, come in all black or all orange. Midis, because of their smaller size and lowered wind resistance, lose velocity less rapidly than standards and hence travel farther before falling. Minis (60 mm) are almost invariably all black. Minis travel extremely rapidly and are quite resistant to being broken.

The *battue* is a thin target with a low-domed top. In the early parts of its course and until it reaches the apex of its travel, the battue flies horizontally and presents its thin edge to the shooter. It is extremely difficult to break or even to see in this position. Because of their low resistance and considerable mass, battues fly very rapidly and lose speed gradually. As the target does slow, it begins to turn slowly, presenting more of its top or round profile to the shooter (this is called development of the target). Battues are very sensitive to wind conditions. At its apex, the battue turns and falls in a slow rolling, arcing curve with its broad face to the shooter; it gains speed as it falls.

The *rabbit* is a thicker version of the standard target, designed to roll along the ground without breaking. Sometimes these targets are termed foxes, geese, etc. Typically, a rabbit rolling along the ground changes speed and/or rises vertically into the air at a moment's notice. Perhaps one of the few constant features of rabbits is that they are constantly variable in their presentation. The thickness of these targets makes them hard to break.

The *rocket*, seldom used in this country but frequently on the European continent, is a 110-mm target similar to a rabbit but with ridges on its top. This construction means that rockets are very hard to break on edge. The rocket leaves the trap extremely rapidly but slows quickly in flight. Like the battue, it flies on edge until it reaches the apex of its flight, where it begins a rapid and almost vertical descent.

Exercises:

1. List the six major types of targets thrown in sporting clays and the key flight characteristics of each.

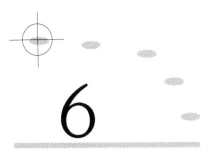

6

SEEING THE TARGET

The first variable in seeing the target clearly is the shooter's eyesight and eyewear. We recommend that a shooter use plastic safety glasses, which should be prescription if the shooter has a visual deficit. We recommend that the glasses be tinted to bring out the target best against the background (Table 6.1) (see also Chapter 14). Since blue waves of light are long and make focusing difficult, blue-blocking orange or yellow lenses can be useful to promote focusing on the target. Third, we recommend you use the palest lenses possible in order to let in the most light; this will constrict your pupils maximally and thus give the maximum depth of focus.

The first consideration in viewing the target is to see the target itself. Target color or colors become an important part of this, along with background. In most situations, the all-orange target is easiest to see. A yellow target thrown against a green background or a black target thrown against a dark background are much more difficult to see. An orange-domed target with a black rim, when viewed from the side, may be particularly confusing because of the black ring against a dark background, but the contrast of orange and black does allow one to bring the orange-domed targets into sharper focus. It has been observed that higher scores are shot

TABLE 6.1 Uses of Various Lens Color

Lens Color	Useful Backgrounds
Target Orange/Yellow	Sky, particularly when overcast
Vermilion/Orange/Bronze	Clear sky
Purple	Green or dark background

with orange-domed targets, as opposed to the all-orange targets on the same stations.

A key variable is weather. Obviously, one can see targets best on a bright, clear day, except when one looks into the sun. On the other hand, patches of sun plus shadows can cause uneven localization of targets. Although targets, even all-orange ones, are difficult to see on drizzly, misty, or foggy days, more consistent scores are shot on these days, presumably because of evenness in viewing the targets throughout the day.

One of the most important parts of any well-designed course is visual barriers to the target. The target that is clearly seen but disappears completely and comes back into view may be erroneously read. It is often better on these targets to pick them up at the point where they become clearly visible for the second time. If the flight path of the target is predictable, one can begin tracking the bird in its first visible segment and depend on one's own sense of timing and rhythm to continue one's gun motions through to the second visible spot. A target passing through the sun, a target passing through shade, or a black target passing against an extremely black background can disappear for a few milliseconds.

When one has observed the target carefully, one needs to begin to make judgments about its speed, angle, fall, and distance. Visual cues from the background and surroundings of the target are particularly helpful because they serve as frames of reference. Some of the most difficult birds are those seen entirely against only clear sky and the horizon, so the shooter has no visual cues. Ideally, one uses the trees, the station, the far side of the shooting field, the trap, the ground between the shooter and the target, *and* between

TABLE 6.2 *Some Optical Illusions*

Situation	**Effect**
Bird travels above or below shooter	Bird appears falsely high
Mini or midi target	Bird appears falsely far
Quartering bird flies from front to behind or from behind to front of shooter	Speed is misjudged *after clay crosses in front of shooter*
Bird's flight is seen against a strong natural line that does not run true	Height or distance misjudged

the shooter and the far side of the shooting field to help establish path of the clay.

One of the major problems in establishing flight path of the clay accurately is the combination of difficulties described above such as light, weather, lack of visual cues, visual barriers, etc. The other major problem is optical illusions created by inappropriately reading the targets against background. One of the most beguiling of optical illusions is that created by terrain that slopes. One has a tremendous tendency to look at the terrain and interpret it as horizontal. For example, a target that is actually falling may appear level when viewed against a rising hill. Even trickier is when the flight path of the bird lies parallel to the slope of the land; in this case, it is very easy to believe that the target is traveling horizontally when it is actually falling. Another excellent example is the target that is traveling beneath the shooter but well above the land. Assessment of target height in this context is extremely difficult. Another example is the bird that is thrown along a hedge or fence, for example, but at a slight angle to it. The natural tendency of the shooter is to perceive that the bird is traveling parallel and horizontal to this visual guide rather than away or down from it. A bird that quarters in or away from the stand creates an illusion of change in speed when the bird crosses in front of the stand. The bird appears to change speed considerably when the shooter perceives that the clay is moving in a different direction in relation to the stand. Similarly, one member of a pair that cross can appear to change speed or direction.

We estimate that typically twenty to forty percent of shots at sporting clays present optical illusions. If you judge that a shot does not present an optical illusion, proceed as outlined in this and in subsequent chapters. If the target does present an optical illusion, you must take a different approach. Your natural instincts will fail you in the case of an optical illusion because the images presented by your eye to your brain are not correct. To overcome this, recognize how to take that particular shot and the differences between where you must actually take it and where your instincts tell you to take it. Program your subconscious computer in advance of stepping into the stand as to what to do. Carry this out. This is described in detail in Chapter 9.

Judging distance accurately, in the best of circumstances, is, unfortunately, an ability many shooters do not possess. We strongly recommend that you develop your own innate sense of accurate distance judgment. Your eye, when trained, can be much more accurate than most range finders. On several of your favorite shooting courses, place a set of stakes at ten-yard intervals. From a variety of positions and angles, learn how to count distance in units of ten yards. Practice this skill repeatedly.

Let's put all this together now with what we learned in Chapter 4: to determine the sweet spot, accurately analyze the true path, speed, and distance of the target; do not be misled by any of the variables discussed above. For example, if you saw a full-orange target on a clear day thrown across a football field, you would see the target clearly and use the ten-yard lines on the field to determine distance.

On the clay course, we must take all variables into account to get that same accurate reading. First of all, judge distance. Use all the visual cues available, plus your ability to judge distance. Factor in the size of the target. A midi thrown at the same distance as a standard target will appear to be more distant; a mini will appear even farther away from the shooter. Take into account the terrain over which the target travels, and establish the flight of the target *against the true horizontal* rather than against the lie of the land. Make a relative judgment about whether the target is fast, slow, or in between. Judge how much of the bird you can actually see to determine the necessary impact of the shot to break the target. Define the sweet spot. Put all these variables together, and construct a map similar to those sketched in Chapter 2. Lastly, remember that no matter how skilled and experienced you are in reading targets, your eye can mislead you because of optical illusions.

Bringing the Target Into Focus

We typically use only about twelve percent of our visual capacity to identify objects. For example, we read signs on the road or passages in a book by looking at the words — not at the individual letters. In other words, most of our day-to-day vision depends upon pattern recognition, which does not require bringing individual objects into sharper focus. The exception is when we coordinate hand-eye movement and motion to perform a task. A perfect example is driving a nail. If you focus your eye on the nail and bring it into sharp focus, the hammer will instinctively hit the nail and not your thumb. As another example, you catch a baseball or softball when you bring the ball into focus. Your hand will be there at the right place and time to catch it, and you never see the glove.

When you bring an object into sharp focus, you use all of your visual and mental skills to determine the spatial location of that object — particularly its place in time (that is, its motion). Think of a stock-car race. As long as you look at the pack, you do not see separate cars, even when you're looking right at them. When you focus on one car and you identify old #43, you identify the many logos on that car at the same time. The car also appears to slow down — briefly. You have brought that car into focus and identified distance, speed, and direction precisely; the act of focusing has also brought out details on the object you hadn't noticed before.

Remember that your time of concentrated focus is quite limited. Look at an object about twenty feet away and bring it into sharp focus. All of a sudden, the details will appear crisp. This will last for only a few tenths of a second. Repeat that experiment using your finger. Identify an object across the room. Look with a blank gaze with your finger pointed at the general direction. Now point directly at the precise object you've previously identified. *Your finger will point at that object at the exact time that you have brought it into focus.*

Instinctive shotgun shooting is basically development and use of this skill. The smooth and effective mount of an accurately fitted gun permits it to become *an extension of your pointing forefinger.* Your hands, eyes, and gun all become one and, in turn, become one with the target. Harnessing this natural and powerful ability is the key to successful wing shooting.

As described in Chapter 3, our method of shooting depends on first identifying the *sweet spot* or optimum place of breaking the target. Second, identify the visual hold point so you can bring the clay into focus at the sweet spot. Third, when the target crosses the visual hold point begin to track the target with your eyes, point to the target with your forearm hand, and begin the mount. When these tasks are successfully completed, you will have a mounted gun pointed directly at the target that is in focus and in the sweet spot. This is instinctive shooting.

Try this. Have a friend at the gun club step about twenty-five feet from you. Have him take an orange target and throw it about twenty-five feet into the air. The target should rise like a teal. On the first target, simply note the flight path. What details on the target did you observe? Now look at a target closely and identify the writing/symbols in the very center; for example, look at the center ring or carve a small black dot in the center. Have your friend throw a second target. Try to identify when the black spot or center ring comes into focus for the first time. For most people, this will be about two-thirds of the height of the target. Have your friend throw a third target. After you've lost the focus the first time, see how many times you can bring it back into focus. Many people will do this twice — at the apex and somewhere on the fall. This is not only a good demonstration of bringing a target into focus but is an excellent exercise for training your eyes to bring moving targets into focus. Play back your visual memories of the target's flight. You should have noticed that every time you brought the black spot into sharp focus the target appeared to become larger and move slower — for a fraction of a second.

As you go around the clay course from now on, try this exercise on every target you can. You can readily bring each target into focus as determined by increased size and slower speed. Next, prove to yourself that the point at which you bring the target into focus is variable. For every target, depending on its distance and speed, a certain interval lies between the point at which the target enters your peripheral vision and the point at which you bring it into focus.

Exercises:

1. What type of glasses do you wear when shooting? Are they safety glasses? Are the tinting and degree of light blocking appropriate for clay shooting?

2. List as many optical illusions as you can that can confuse you about the true read of a target.

3. Have you practiced judging distance?

4. Have you practiced bringing a wide variety of targets into focus?

7

SHOT STREAMS AND PATTERNS

Shot emerges from the barrel of the gun as a small but rapidly expanding cylinder. Depending on the weight, size, and number of shot, the powder load, and the mechanics of the load, the cylinder of shot rapidly expands parallel to its distance of travel so that it becomes an elongated oval termed the shot stream. Depending on these variables plus the choke, the shot column also expands laterally as it moves from the gun.

The standard way of measuring the progressive lateral/vertical dispersion of shot is to use a pattern board. Typically, the shooter fires one to five shells at a fixed point on a soft board while standing forty yards in front of the board. On the board, a thirty-inch circle is then drawn. The number of pellets that land within the circle are counted. The circle is drawn before the shot is fired. The percentage of the total numbers of that shot that fall within the circle is called the pattern efficiency. Depending on the choke, a variable number of pellets will strike within the thirty-inch circle at forty yards.

The dispersion of shot at right angles to the line of pellet flight has also been assessed by pulling a moving target throughout the shot column at a predetermined distance. This assesses the size/

density of the shot stream from its beginning to its end. Typically, a shot stream may be three to four feet high and eight to fifteen feet long. In approximately the middle of the shot column, the greatest density of shot, as viewed from beginning to end of the column, is generally observed. These matters are described in Bob Brister's book *Shotgunning, The Art and the Science*. In his testing, Brister found wide variations in shot streaming between various chokes, loads, shot sizes, gauges, powders, loading conditions, and distances. Of interest, the percentage of pellets in the shot stream, when viewed from beginning to end, that were located within the thirty-inch circle of maximum density ranged from twenty percent to ninety percent. This thirty-inch circle was located approximately in the center of the column.

Here, we summarize the features of shot stream we think important. First, the number or density of shot contained within a thirty-inch circle will be optimum at a given distance when one uses a particular choke and shell (Figure 2.1). Second, the shot do not travel as a wall or even a sphere but rather as a complex stream of shot. Third, shot number and density are not evenly distributed throughout the stream but are more heavily weighted toward the center of the shot stream. Lastly, significant gaps or holes can occur, particularly in the latter parts of the shot stream, so that the shooter may have actually aimed the gun correctly but the target evades breakage by slipping through a hole in the pattern. Accordingly to Oberfell and Thompson, a one-and-one-eighth-ounce load of #7$\frac{1}{2}$ shot (three hundred and ninety three pellets) patterning at an efficiency of fifty percent will be likely to have three patches devoid of pellets of five-inch diameter within the thirty-inch circle. This number would rise to ten if patterning efficiency fell to twenty-five percent. Remember that when one patterns a shotgun at a given distance, one sees the vertical and lateral displacement of *the entire shot column* and that one determines efficiency of localization within a thirty-inch circle. If one considers that, in relationship to a moving target, that thirty-inch circle is really a three-dimensional thirty-inch sphere, the efficiency of location *within this sphere* will obviously be considerably less than that measured by the thirty-inch circle. In sum, one depends upon the density and evenness of pattern in this thirty-inch sphere to break targets and kill birds. To us, this points up the need for accurate delivery of the shot sphere and for use of tighter chokes.

Practical implications of these considerations are as follows. First, one should select the choke appropriate for the distance from the shooter to the point at which the target is to be broken. Second, one gains a certain minimum advantage in the fact that the shot stream is elongated, because that potentially increases your chances of having the target pass through the path of the shot stream. This potential advantage is offset by the fact that the latter portions of the shot stream may well be of insufficient density to break the target. For these and other reasons, we recommend (see Chapter 2) that one should use a tighter choke than distance of the target per se would dictate. It is better to use a tighter choke and deliver the shot stream accurately than to depend on the width/length of the shot column to make a poor shot into a hit.

Exercise:

1. Draw a typical shot stream. Show some approximate dimensions and where the greatest of concentration of shot will fall.

8

LEAD AND BIRD-BARREL RELATIONSHIP

Lead

A target moving at sixty mph is crossed by a stream of shot moving approximately seven hundred mph. Assume a target forty yards from the shooter. The shot travels 1200 FPS. The shot will require one-tenth of a second to reach the target. In this period of time, the target will have traveled about nine feet (eighty-eight FPS). If we shot directly at the target, we would have delivered the shot nine feet behind the target. To overcome this problem, shotgunners have developed a variety of methods of delivering in front of the bird.

Over the years, five basic types of lead have been developed. The first of these, widely used almost exclusively in skeet as well as in long shots on game, is *maintained or sustained lead*. In this method, the shooter inserts the gun into the path of the bird in front of the clay. He establishes the appropriate lead for the bird by assessing the relationship between barrel and bird; he sustains this lead until confident he has fully achieved it. He then delivers and continues to move the gun as he had done before. The second method is the classic technique of wing shooting, which is called *pass through or pull through.* In this method, the shooter inserts on or behind the bird. He pulls the gun through the bird and he delivers the shot at the moment his instincts deem appropriate. His instincts have told him to deliver at a point that will give sufficient lead. Lead is usually controlled by rapid acceleration of the gun swing, just before delivery. A third method of lead was developed by the London gunmaker and shooter Robert Churchill. The essence of the *Churchilian method* is that one's natural instincts accurately determine lead. In his method, one completes the mount of the gun on the bird and at that instant delivers. A fourth and recently popularized method by John Bidwell involves the use of maintained lead. In this method, the gun is inserted in front of the target. One depends on one's natural instinct to maintain the appropriate distance between barrel and bird without looking at the gun. Lastly, there is the *pull-away method.* In this method, the shooter mounts in front of the bird. Rather than maintaining a sustained lead, he actively pulls away at considerably increased speed, as in the follow-through method, to establish appropriate lead.

Each of these methods has many adherents and each has its own inherent advantages and disadvantages. The classic sustained lead is difficult to adapt to sporting clays because it requires extensive recognition of barrel position. One is not therefore bringing the bird into focus because one tends to focus back and forth *between the bird and the barrel.* We recommend a method that uses some features of the Churchillian and follow-through methods. We believe, however, that we can define the instinctive part of when to deliver more precisely. We have observed John Bidwell shoot, and in his hands his method of maintained lead is highly successful. The classic pull-away method depends upon instinct to determine lead (which we believe can be better defined) and inserts the gun barrel in front of the bird (which we believe leads to lessened control of the gun and lessened hand-eye coordination).

The method we recommend is basically a pull-through or a pull-away method, where we have analyzed in some detail and established in a rational way the principles and procedures needed to establish and to control precisely the degree of necessary lead. The pull-through or pull-away is tightly controlled in several ways. An essential purpose of this book is to teach the clay shooter how to apply these principles and methods to understand and employ our method effectively. The basic scenario is to insert on or behind the bird and pull-through; it is useful for all but the longest of leads. Typically, pull-through will therefore provide sufficient lead on anything up to a crossing bird at more than thirty yards. With leads greater than this, a modification of our method that employs pull-away will be described later in this chapter.

Controlled Pull-Through

We recommend insertion of the gun at a variable length behind the target. Then, begin swinging the gun slightly faster than the speed of the bird (one mile an hour faster). Pull through the target and deliver when your instincts tell you to do so. The visual cues to deliver automatically are: 1) when the barrel of the gun (recognized but not seen in focus) crosses the target, 2) when your eyes bring the target into focus. Our instincts tell us at this point that *we must deliver the shot* and we will. In fact, we may shoot way over, below, in front of, or behind the bird when we receive that cue. Control of pull-through consequently lies in *establishing the correct path and speed of gun movement in relationship to the path and speed of the bird and in mounting and inserting the gun at the correct place before the visual cue for delivery is given.* After the cue is given, we have a greatly reduced ability to deliver voluntarily, though we can do so if we program our computer in advance (see Chapter 9).

If we insert a good distance behind the bird (let's say one foot maximum) and begin moving the gun slightly faster, the visual cue is delivered almost as soon as the barrel reaches the bird. This means that the amount of lead delivered is minimal. On the other hand, if we insert right on the bird and begin moving the gun slightly faster, we will be well past the target before the visual cue takes effect. This will produce maximum lead. *One of the essential control points is use of the correct insertion point.*

We have repeatedly recommended focusing on the target to promote the most effective hand-eye coordination, but there is another reason for doing so. Think of the target as an object the size of a grapefruit. If we focus on that as our visual cue, our natural tendency will be to point the gun *at the grapefruit*. If we have not brought the target into sharp focus but have pulled through it, we will see the target as a large sphere — say the size of a garbage can lid. Yet, pulling through this lid plus bringing the target to subsequent focus will provide the visual cue for delivery. Thus, you will point the gun anywhere within the radius of the garbage can lid at delivery. Not surprisingly, when you have not focused on a target, your shot stream will tend to miss it. It is hitting in the garbage can lid you aimed at but that may or may not include the grapefruit that you really want. *Focusing on the bird at delivery is a second key control point in this method.*

The classic reason for not focusing on the bird is looking at the barrel. When you do this, you don't look at the bird *or* at the barrel. Rather, you look at a spot between the two. Have your friend hold up both fists three to four feet apart. Look at them both. Where are you focused? (Answer: between them). Let's think about that in terms of a shot. If your focal point is between the barrel and the bird, you will deliver when the barrel passes through the focal point. Your instincts will tell you to put the gun barrel on the focal point and you will shoot between the bird and the barrel. The following has happened to each of us. We get a close pair. We miss and don't know why. Your buddy says you shot between them. What happened? You didn't focus on either bird but, in fact, were trying to see both. Your focal point lay between the birds, and that's where you shot. This not only changes where you shoot but your perception of distance as well (the change will appear closer).

How do we in fact establish lead or bird-barrel relationship for a given shot? The answer is we don't — at least not while we're shooting. While you're shooting, your entire energy should be concentrated upon focusing on the bird. You have set up a plan before entering the stand on how or where to hold, where to pick up the bird, and where to insert. Carry out the plan and keep all of your attention on the target and on bringing it to focus at the sweet spot. Trust your instincts as to when to deliver. When you have completed the shot, *then tap your subconscious and play the shot back.* Ask yourself where you were when you delivered. Do this whether you hit the shot or not. You will find that you can establish from your subconscious where your gun barrel was at the moment of delivery easily for misses and incomplete breaks. Use this information to make the next shot better. We've mentioned before that it is very hard to access your computer when you've delivered a really solid hit. Now you understand why. A really solid hit means that the bird, your hands, gun, and eyes all came together at one precise moment in an instinctive and incredibly powerful but controlled event. When that occurs, the instinct is hard to reconstruct from your computer because it all happens so naturally and rapidly. When you have tried this a few times, you'll begin to recognize how incredibly pure and sweet a solid hit really is.

Establishing Lead in Controlled Follow-Through

Three basic variables determine the extent of lead: distance of target, speed of target, and angle of target. The farther the target, the greater amount of lead necessary. This is obvious from the foregoing. As distance to the target increases, the farther the target can travel in the interval between pulling the trigger and arrival of the shot stream at the target, and so the greater the lead. For similar reasons, greater target speed equals greater lead. Lastly, angle helps to determine lead. A crossing target at a perfect right angle to the shooter requires the maximum amount of lead. Imagine a line running straight to the target from the shooter at 180° or toward twelve o'clock. Then, imagine a line at 90° line running from three o'clock to nine o'clock. This represents a perfect crosser. The

TABLE 8.1 Key Points for Establishing Lead in Controlled Follow-Through

1. Accurate determination of required lead.
2. Insertion of gun at appropriate point on path of bird.
3. Bringing bird into focus at time of delivery.

closer a quartering bird comes to the six o'clock-twelve o'clock axis, the less lead is necessary; the closer it comes to the three o'clock-nine o'clock axis, the greater the lead. The total amount of lead is determined by the sum of these three factors (Table 8.1 and Figure 8.1).

We begin to establish estimated lead by making a rough estimate of these three factors. Observe the speed, distance, and angle of the bird carefully and be sure that you have made these judgments accurately. Assess whether the bird falls in one of the

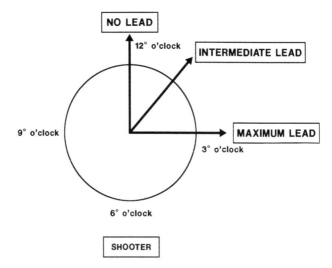

Figure 8.1 Effects of angle between shooter and path of bird on amount of lead. A bird going directly away from or toward the shooter requires no horizontal lead, while a bird crossing at ninety degrees requires the maximum amount of lead. Quartering birds, whether incoming or outgoing, obviously require intermediate leads.

TABLE 8.2 *Factors Determining Lead*

Factor	Effect
Speed	↑ Speed ---> ↑ Lead
Angle	Closer to 90° ---> ↑ Lead
Distance	↑ Distance ---> ↑ Lead

categories (such as a bird above or below the shooter) where distance and angle can be deceiving. From these, make a rough estimate of whether the lead will be small, moderate, or large. The largest amount of lead will be required by a fast bird that is a long distance from the shooter and traveling at right angles to the shooter. The smallest amount of lead will be required by a close-in target (say at twenty yards), quartering almost directly away from the shooter and traveling at slow speed.

The judgment of required lead or of how to use that information is not an exact or quantitative science. One can begin by establishing whether the lead is likely to be very long, long, intermediate, or short. For a short lead, insert the gun during the mount well behind the bird (that is, insert the muzzle about eight inches behind the clay). For an intermediate lead, try three to four inches. For a long lead, try barely behind the bird. For maximum lead, insert directly on the center of the bird. It is important that, having inserted the gun, you move the gun at a speed slightly faster than the bird and that you follow through after delivery. If you don't follow through for a few feet, you will stop the gun. Fortunately, your subconscious computer can make extensive corrections to overcome mistakes in this program.

A key step in the method is analyzing each shot (whether a hit or a miss) and taking appropriate actions based on that analysis to improve the next shot. A popular saying at many gun clubs is, "Man, you've really dialed that shot in." What is meant by that is that the shooter has arrived at an optimum synthesis of gaze point, gun-hold point, insertion point, and sweet spot so that he breaks the target easily and cleanly. After each shot that is not a perfect hit, adjust one or more of these variables to improve what you are doing.

Let's take an example. You're shooting at a twenty-yard crosser that is moving fairly fast. You've determined that the amount of lead needed is moderate and you've inserted about three inches behind the bird. After you deliver, you observe that you missed. Reach into your subconscious computer and play back the tape of that shot. *Where were you at the point of delivery?* Your computer tells you that you were on the line of flight of the bird but slightly behind it. That is, you did not have enough lead. You try the shot again but this time you insert about one to two inches behind the clay. You hit the butt of the bird. You replay and you are just barely on the clay. The third time, you insert right on the butt of the bird and get a clean break. You have now dialed in that shot.

This is one of the key steps in our method. First, doing this improves accuracy on each shot at the same bird. You now have an established method for learning how to hit any bird. In terms of score, you can improve throughout a given stand, so missing the first bird or two does not mean that you will miss all of them. Second, you program your computer. Your subconscious computer contains a large amount of hand-eye memory. If you can learn to hit a particular crosser consistently, that information is stored in your computer. You will have a memory of how to analyze the shot, where to insert, how to make the moves, how to pull through, and when to deliver. When you confront a similar bird in the future, your subconscious memory will make that hit for you easily. You can tap that data base to help you shoot better consistently. This is one reason why we recommend rapidly establishing good gun fit and shooting the same shell. If you do not program your computer consistently, it will not give you consistent answers.

The most sensitive step in this method is insertion of the gun. There are at least two common errors at this point. The first is taking your eyes off the bird. You don't need to see the hood of your car to drive through difficult traffic, and you don't need to see the barrel of the gun, *in your conscious mind*, to insert it at the proper point. The second major error is stopping or slowing motion of the hands. This obviously completely disrupts hand-eye coordination and invariably leads to a miss. The major reason for stopping the gun is looking at the barrel. When we become consciously aware of our barrel, that signals our body that our focus has shifted from the target to a spot between gun and target. The body's natural response is to put on brakes and stop what it is doing until the eyes begin to focus on a new target and the mind reestablishes the desired gun path. During this down time, your gun stops and you have lost coordination with the target. As discussed above, you are also very liable to deliver at this point because your barrel has passed through the place where you are seeing the target. Other errors include canted barrel, slumped head, and misalignment of barrel with line of sight.

Let's take a practical example. Have a friend stand about twenty feet from you and throw a target into the air. Try to focus on the center ring. Now pick up your shotgun and look at the bead. Look down the barrel and concentrate on the bead. Try to put the bead on the dark spot. Have your friend observe your gun motion. He or she will report to you that it is a series of jerky stops and starts.

The most practical application of the foregoing is this: No method of establishing lead in dynamic clay-target shooting can be successful if it requires you to judge consciously the distance between barrel and bird. As soon as you are consciously measuring lead, your eyes focus on the space between the target and the gun. You are not reading the true angle, speed, and distance of the bird, and you are telling your body to deliver not on the target but on a space between the target and the barrel.

Complex Leads

A complex lead is one that requires that the gun must move ahead of the clay in two dimensions—vertically and horizontally. In a simple and level crosser, lead is only in one dimension, horizontal

(Figure 8.2A). In this case, the direction or vector of lead is horizontal and parallel to flight of the bird. When targets are rising/falling (at say 45°) as well as traveling laterally, lead in two dimensions is

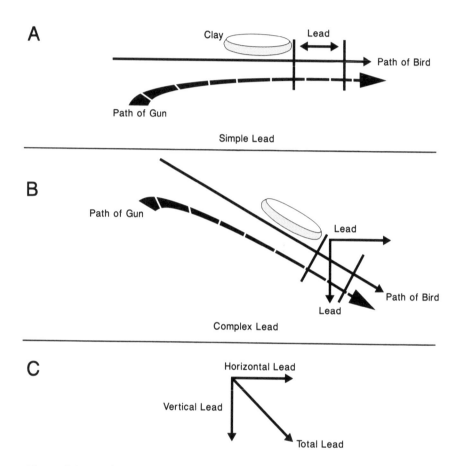

Figure 8.2 Simple and complex lead. In panel A, simple lead is depicted. The gun barrel travels parallel not only to the flight of the bird but to the ground. In this case, only front lead is required. In panel B is depicted complex lead. Here, the gun barrel travels parallel to the path of the bird but at an angle to the ground — the true standard of reference. Thus, the target is both moving forward and falling downward. Lead thus has two dimensions (i.e., it is complex). The actual amount of lead, which will be determined by your subconscious computer, lies at a forward and downward angle in relation to the ground and parallel to the actual flight of the bird. In mathematical terms, lead represents the sum of the two (i.e., horizontal and vertical) vectors. The sum of the vectors is shown in panel 8.2C.

needed (Figure 8.2B). Although the complex lead requires two dimensions, the total or vector of lead is in one direction and that again lies *parallel* to flight of the bird (Figure 8.2C). The key to establishing complex lead is to follow the bird with the barrel in parallel to the clay's flight path (Figure 8.2C). Your subconscious computer, if given half a chance, will establish the most complex of leads for you.

Controlled Pull-Away

The basic method of lead described so far, controlled pull-through, is good for all but the longest of leads. As a practical example, this method will be successful on the lead for anything up to a crossing bird at thirty to thirty-two yards. Beyond that, we recommend a somewhat different method of establishing lead.

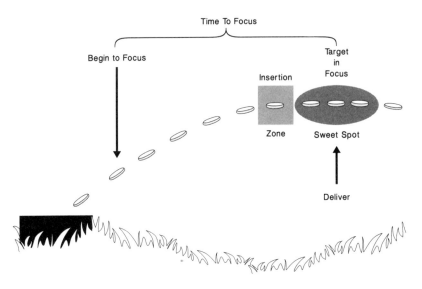

Figure 8.3 Insertion zone and time to focus for long leads. Note that the insertion zone still lies behind the sweet spot and that the bird is brought into focus at the sweet spot.

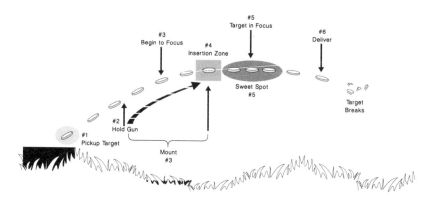

Figure 8.4 Key points in controlled pull-away.

Lead, when we move the gun only slightly faster than the clay, is established basically by the interval of time between: 1) when we insert the gun, and 2) when our instincts tell us to deliver—cued principally by our bringing the barrel through the clay and the target into focus. Even when one inserts the barrel directly onto the front of the target, there is a maximum amount of time before the target will come into focus and hence a maximum amount of lead that can be produced by inserting on or behind the clay (see Figure 3.3). For leads requiring a distance greater than that, one needs to modify the method.

The fundamental to be modified is *where to insert the gun*. For longer leads, we insert the gun *in front of the bird* at increasing distances for increasing lead (Figure 8.3). We call this method *controlled pull-away*. Save for the exact insertion point, the basic principles of controlled pull-away are the same as for controlled pull-through (Figure 8.4). When you see the blur of the target, begin your mount by pointing. Develop the mount and, at the appropriate spot, begin to focus on the clay. At the same time that you insert, move the barrel slightly faster than the clay and bring the clay into focus — without looking at the barrel (Figure 8.4). Our subconscious, as in the controlled pull-through method, estimates the distance between the barrel and the bird and makes a correct judgment. In this method, as in controlled pull-through, do not consciously judge either the insertion point or lead. At the appropriate moment — cued mainly by bringing the target into focus — we will deliver and hence establish a longer and more appropriate lead.

The sweet spot is where it would be in controlled pull-through. For a thirty-five-yard crossing bird, insert the barrel about six inches in front of the bird; for a forty-five-yard crossing bird, insert the barrel about twelve inches; and for a sixty-yard crossing bird, insert the barrel about two feet (Figure 8.5). For quartering birds, insert closer to the clay because the lead on these birds is less (see

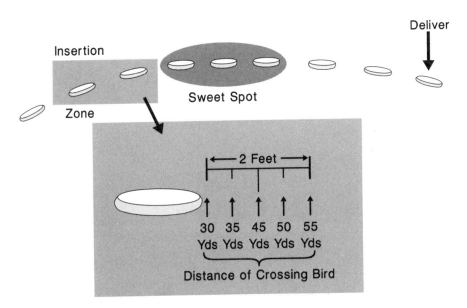

Figure 8.5 Amount of insertion required for birds at various distances in controlled pull-away. Here we are depicting a crossing bird (which requires a maximum lead) at distances of thirty to fifty-five yards). Insert from right on the beak of the bird to two feet in front of it. Increase speed slightly, pull away, and deliver when the target comes into focus. Less lead will be necessary for quartering birds.

Figure 8.1). This method has been used successfully by duck and goose hunters for many years on long crossing or overhead shots.

To summarize the method of controlled pull-away, select the sweet spot. Then select the point of beginning to focus on the clay so that the target will come into focus at the sweet spot. Call for the target and pick up its blur. Begin to focus and begin to move the gun as described previously (see Chapter 4). Insert the gun (six to twenty-four inches) ahead of the clay in the insertion zone. Increase gun speed slightly. When you pull through the target and bring the clay into focus, you will deliver. Use your subconscious computer to analyze the shot and make any needed corrections.

Exercises:

1. Define five basic types of lead.
2. Define controlled pull-through as a method for establishing lead.
3. Highlight the major differences between this and the other five forms of lead.
4. What three conditions of the target most affect lead? How does each of these change lead?
5. Define in your own words "Dialing in a shot." Lay out step by step a plan for dialing in a given shot.
6. Describe when and how to use complex lead.
7. Describe when and how to use controlled pull-through.

9

YOUR SUBCONSCIOUS AS A COMPUTER

The human mind is capable of achieving truly wonderful things. We are a long way from complete artificial intelligence. As a practical example, your eye can sort out complex two- and three-dimensional patterns far better than the computer-driven systems now available.

One of the most powerful parts of our mind is our subconscious. Many things we see daily are recorded and acted upon by the subconscious, of which we are not aware. For example, much of driving a car is an almost subconscious and instinctive action (automatic pilot). Most of us are capable of doing other things while we drive. Many of us can sit at our desk and run a calculator, computer, or video game and talk on the telephone as these activities are conducted by our subconscious. We hasten to add that the subconscious we refer to is associated with our conscious mind and represents a compartmentalization of activity, rather than the subconscious as described by Freud.

You can tap your subconscious to help you analyze shots. You don't even need to be at the gun club to do this. Remember that frustrating target you struggled with last week but didn't hit? Play back, *at slow motion*, where your barrel was when you delivered the shot in relation to the target. If you were shooting correctly, you were not conscious of where your barrel was when you delivered. If you missed, a mental picture will form of precisely where the barrel was in relationship to the bird. You were over it, under it, behind it, etc. Think of the other shots in that series. If you can remember them clearly, you will not get exactly the same visual pattern for each shot.

This is an important ability of your subconscious. Practice using it. The umpire at home plate frequently does not make an immediate call on a tough force from third. He steps back from the plate. What is he doing? He's replaying the event and trying to assess where the ball was, where the catcher was, and where the extended leg of the runner was in relation to home plate. Practice this skill every time you're at the gun club. On every shot, ask yourself where your barrel was when you delivered and you will soon be able to do this readily. Remember: The targets you break the best will be the most difficult to remember.

You can use your subconscious further. *You can program it in advance of a shot.* Normally when we take a shot, we deliver when the barrel pulls through the bird and we bring the target into focus. If our eye misreads the target's flight path, we must deliver *on the true path of the target and not on the perceived path if we are to break the target.* You can program your subconscious to do this. Let's take a tower shot that's quartering away rapidly. Because the target is above us, its fall is difficult to judge. Our eye may mislead us, and we may well believe that the target is traveling flat when it actually is falling considerably. When we shoot by pulling through the target on its perceived path, we will actually be shooting over the target. The remedy for this is to shoot lower. Before stepping into the stand, tell your subconscious that you do not want to shoot on the path but below it by an approximate amount. This is your basic plan of attack. Try this and you'll be pleasantly surprised. It will take a few shots to get familiar. But when you start hitting the target and playing back those hits, you will find that you have not delivered where your instincts told you. Rather, your subconscious has told you to move beyond and below the bird and then deliver. Congratulations! You have successfully programmed your computer.

This is one of the key elements in our method of shooting. We estimate that approximately sixty to eighty percent of the targets can be read accurately by the eye and can be taken by a pure instinctive approach. The other twenty to forty percent present optical illusions that mislead the eye. We must shoot, not where our eye tells us is right, but at a predetermined different spot. We do this by programming our subconscious before we step into the stand.

Remember that the basis of our method for all shots is that the target must be brought into sharp, concentrated focus at the time of the shot. You must not be looking at anything else. If you are consciously aware of anything but the target at the moment of delivery, you have likely predetermined that you will miss.

Exercises:

1. Replay five different shots at different stands you made the last time you shot sporting clays.

2. The next time you go to the gun club, practice replaying each shot on a stand for five different stands — after you have left the stand.

10

HOW TO HOLD AND MOUNT THE GUN

Holding the Gun

The hand gripping the forearm is the power/action hand for gun mount. Grasp the forearm using a three-finger grip. Place the little, ring, and middle fingers on one side of the forearm. Place the thumb on the other. Place the index finger along the barrel so that it points exactly as the barrel points. Grasp the forearm *firmly*.

Use the other hand to grasp the stock. Place the index finger around the trigger. Be sure that the first joint of the trigger finger is placed on the trigger. Unlike a rifle where the trigger is pressed by the forefinger, the shotgun shooter uses the first joint of the index finger against the trigger to get the quickest, most effective pull. To increase control of the stock, place the thumb around the stock and press on the stock rather than placing it on top as in the hunting position. Use of the safety is not necessary because in clays we keep the gun unbreached at all times when not actually shooting.

In the instinctive method of shooting, the forearm hand is the power/action hand that moves and directs the gun in direct coordination with the eye. The other hand guides and supports the stock. Both the forearm and the stock should be held firmly and tightly.

Do not squeeze tightly, but do use a very firm grip so that the gun is completely under control and does not move except when desired.

Gun Position

We have already discussed how to hold the butt of the stock (Chapter 3). We recommend adopting one uniform hold position suitable for shooting under all types of tournament rules. A good place to hold the stock is at approximately the nipple line. The butt of the gun must be visible under the arm but does not have to be under the arm — in terms of front-to-back or both. In fact, we suggest holding the stock just touching the front of the body so that the gun slides easily into position. Read the official rule books of the NSCA and USSCA to be familiar with the current formal definitions of gun hold.

The most important part of holding the gun is holding the barrel at the proper height. The height of the tip of the barrel is the principal factor in controlling the height of the shot column when you deliver. Imagine a string held between your nose and the height of the target *when it is at the sweet spot*. Hold the tip of the barrel slightly below this line so that you do not impair your view of the target. From this position, you can easily move the gun the appropriate height for taking the bird at the sweet spot.

Hold the gun at the same height on the chest for all shots. Use the forearm hand to raise or lower the tip of the barrel to the appropriate height. Make sure that the barrel does not obstruct your view at any time. Do not cant the gun to either side; hold it directly vertical. You have now set yourself up so that eyes, hands, gun, and target will come together at the sweet spot.

There are two situations where estimating height of the target is particularly difficult: 1) when the bird is traveling beneath the shooter or 2) when the bird is traveling above the shooter. In both cases, you lose visual cues. Imagine an object between you and the ceiling. It is relatively easy to tell that the object is above you and close to the ceiling. It is much more difficult to determine how close the object is to the ceiling. In the same way, a target above or below you can be misjudged. In both cases, one tends to judge the target as actually higher than it is, partially because the target is likely to be falling.

Gun Mount

Let's review some of the key features. Gun mount is an active process which leads to effective barrel, eye, and target interaction. For a fast-moving sport like sporting clays, one is actually at an advantage by using a low gun because you have active movement in the mount. Second, begin with the head erect. Third, the mount begins with a positive pointing of the forearm, hand, and, specifically, the index finger toward the bird. This active pointing is the first part of the mount and is begun slightly before the bird reaches the hold point of the gun. Fourth, this action establishes, from the first, that the movement of the hands, gun, and body are in rhythm with the speed of the bird and therefore sets the flow of the shot. *This is one of the key elements in timing.* Fifth, the mount should be a smooth, rapid, graceful, and integrated whole, beginning with the initial pointing movement and culminating, not in the delivery, but in the follow-through. Insertion to control lead should be essentially a subconscious decision. It is important here, as in all parts of the mount, not to look at the barrel. When insertion is completed, the barrel must be aligned perfectly with the master eye and movement of the barrel should be in rhythm with and at approximately the same speed as the bird. Then, accelerate the gun slightly and pull through the bird. Deliver. Continue the follow-through.

The mount is guided by the forearm hand in coordination with the eye. After the mount is complete, the upper body locks into a whole. Forward motion of the gun is continued by rotation of the upper body on the lower. When the gun is mounted, the barrel must be perfectly aligned with the master eye — vertically and laterally. Make sure that one looks down a barrel or rib that is horizontal and not canted to one side or another; canting is a serious cause of misses. Also, make sure your line of sight is aligned with the barrel. Your natural pointing mechanism will not work if you do not point the barrel where your master eye sees.

The gun barrel should not, unless absolutely necessary, ever obstruct your view of the target. The basic plan of attack is always to hold the gun in position so that at the hold point and throughout its entire travel view of the target is not obstructed.

A final key element is the type of motion. Both economy and smoothness are highly desirable. One should not move the barrel any more than necessary. Usually one needs to move the gun no more than a few inches along the path of the bird and even less vertically. Move the gun as smoothly as possible through the target and during follow-through. Think of *lightly stroking the gun through the target* at a speed only slightly greater than the target.

Don't mount the gun too early. The most effective mount is one where you *mount approximately on the bird*, pull through, and deliver *in one fluid, instinctive motion*. There is a great tendency on a slow bird, particularly an incomer and crosser, to mount too soon and to ride the bird. In this situation, one generally has many opportunities to take the bird. But constantly staying on the bird, one loses a fluid, active mount and tends to measure the bird. The result is all too often a miss.

Exercises:

1. Describe how to hold the gun with both hands.
2. Describe where to hold the gun in relationship to the flight path of the bird.
3. Review the key steps in mounting the gun.

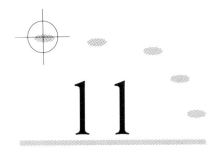

11

TYPES OF SHOTS

Introduction

There are six basic shots in sporting clays. These are: incoming; outgoing; passing; quartering; crossing; and rising/falling. For each of these shots, the consistent use of a few basic principles will make for the easiest hits. Many special shots (such as the rabbit, quail walk, or flush) represent variations on one of these six basic themes. One need only to apply the principles of the basic shot and then consider the special circumstances. In addition, four general modifying conditions can apply to each of the six basic shots, and two others to crossing/quartering shots.

We define an *outgoing or incoming bird* as one going away from or toward the stand, rising or falling, within a ninety-degree arc from 10:30 to 1:30 (Figure 11.1). An *incoming shot*, which frequently flies overhead, may also fly low. A *passing shot* passes over the head of the shooter. A *quartering bird* is an outgoing or incoming bird flying in a ninety-degree arc that extends either from 1:30 to 4:30 or from 7:30 to 10:30, with the exception of those birds that are at ninety-degree or straight right angles (i.e. on an axis from 3:00 to 9:00 to the shooter). These are *crossers*. *Rising/falling* targets travel vertically.

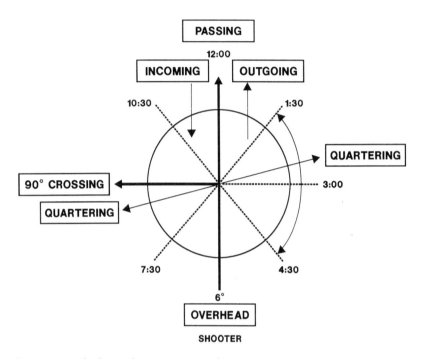

Figure 11.1 The basic shots in sporting clays.

The first modifying principle comes into play when a target flies above or below the shooter. In this case, judgment of height is difficult because the shooter is looking either up or down at the target, often against an indefinite frame of reference. Since most targets are falling (albeit slowly) when taken and since this may be imperceptible, a great tendency to shoot over targets above or below the shooter exists. The second modifying condition is when a battue or rocket is thrown (see Chapter 5). Because of the flight characteristics of the battue, it should be taken at the height of its travel, when it has just rolled over and begun its descent. Its vertical speed will be the lowest then and it will present the largest and most breakable surface to the shooter. The rocket should be taken at the apex of its flight path just as it begins to fall, in order to reduce vertical speed of the target. Third, falling or dropping targets are covered in detail under incomers. The basic principles for taking falling or dropping birds are: a) avoid the situation whenever possible; b) take the bird as high in its descent as possible to minimize speed and; c) pull through the bird and deliver.

A fourth general modification is presented by a distant target — far away, high, or both. First, pay extra attention to judging the necessary lead on these birds because your margin of error will be quite small. Second, use a tight choke, but remember that the pattern efficiency of even a tight choke past forty-five yards falls rapidly. Third, insert on the bird and pull through rapidly. You may need to estimate lead by "dialing the shot in" (see Chapter 8).

Another modifying principle applies particularly to crossing or quartering birds that are not traveling horizontally when taken. Rather, the targets are rising or falling at an angle that may range from shallow to steep. That is, the lead is complex (see Chapter 8). In this case, the gun barrel must track not only the horizontal flight of the bird but its vertical traverse as well. The basic approach to this situation is to establish a gun-hold position which will permit easy tracking of both the vertical and horizontal paths until you deliver.

Let's take an example. You are presented with a twenty-five-yard crosser. If the clay moved only horizontally, you would track the clay only in the horizontal direction (Figure 11.2A). If the bird rises at an angle of forty-five degrees, you should raise the gun barrel, after insertion, in parallel with the rise of the target as well as laterally and move the barrel slightly faster than the target (Figure 11.2B). Pull through and deliver. These maneuvers would apply in reverse to a falling target (Figure 11.2C).

A more complex situation prevails when the target's vertical path breaks between the gun-hold point and the sweet spot. A typical example would be a crossing woodcock (Figure 11.2D). At the point where you hold the gun, the bird is rising. Before the bird reaches the sweet spot, it passes its inflection point and begins to fall. The easiest solution is to reorganize your shot by moving your gun-hold point down the lateral path of the bird. The gun can then sweep down through and parallel to the path of the falling target as above (Figure 11.2C). Physical constraints of the target presentation may, however, not permit this option. If so, select the best gun-hold point in terms of lateral travel needed. Hold the gun *at about the height where you will take the target*. As the target rises and then falls, do not follow its vertical travels. Instead, move your gun laterally in sync with the target as you would for a simple crosser to about the insertion spot. Then pull down *and parallel to* the falling clay, speed up the gun to devote both leads (lateral and bottom), pull through, and deliver (Figure 11.2D).

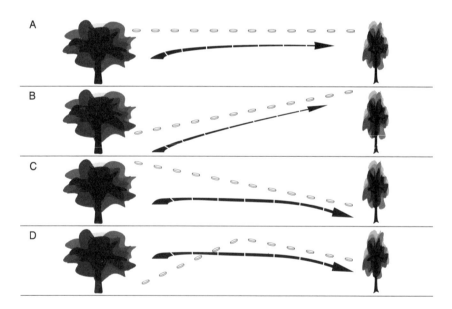

Figure 11.2 Motion of gun barrel in relationship to various target flight paths. In panel A, the target moves horizontally. In panel B, it rises. In panel C, it falls. In panel D, it rises and then falls.

Doubles

When the shooter is presented with a single, a report pair, or a following pair in the shots described below, the same basic strategies apply. True doubles, however, pose certain special difficulties. A pair of doubles will tend to move slower at a lower height because of the increased weight of the two birds. The flight of the two birds will tend to be compressed; that is, the birds will begin to fall earlier in their path and travel a shorter distance. On some traps, members of the pair will not behave similarly. Pairs that cross can appear to change direction or speed.

The key problem in doubles is selecting which bird to take first. The basic principle is to select the bird taken first so that gun movement toward the second bird is: 1) minimal; and 2) in the same direction as that needed to take the first bird. As a general rule, take the lower of the pair first; this will permit you to continue to rise to the second bird. Likewise, take the trailing bird first so that you can continue your swing onto the other. In rising teal, take the bird that peaks first with your first shot.

Immediately after delivering on the first bird, move your eyes to the second bird and pick it up in your peripheral vision. If you see the first bird break, you have kept your eyes on it too long. Begin focusing on the second bird. At the same time, point with your forearm hand toward the second bird. Pull through the second bird and deliver at the appropriate point, which will generally be similar to that used for the first bird. This latter situation may not pertain if the flight characteristics of the two birds are different at the time when they are taken. We have described this situation in detail in the section on straightaways below.

A good general strategy for doubles is to take the first bird a little more quickly than you would a comparable single. Then, after you have delivered and followed through on the first shot, move your eyes to the second bird immediately without seeing the first bird break. *If you have time, it is always advantageous to remount your gun, since this active process gives you more control and helps to coordinate hand-eye instincts for both tracking the bird and delivery.* Once you have moved to the second bird, deliver at the appropriate time even if you perceive that the clay is broken. Don't take the risk of thinking that you have broken the second bird, for the referee may not see it that way.

One of the most difficult decisions in sporting clays is determining which of a pair, launched from different traps, to take first. First, analyze each bird carefully and determine the sweet spot for each independently. Sometimes, this alone will dictate your choice of which target to take. For example, one target may leave the shooting field quickly (by falling to the ground, passing behind an obstruction, breaking on a tree, etc.) before the other. Next, take that bird first that will give you the best chance of minimizing gun movement for the second. You may wish to consider taking the right-handed bird first, if you are right-handed (the left-handed bird first if you are left-handed). A right-handed shooter, after mounting his gun, can see a left target easier than a right.

When you have determined the bird to take first, selecting the sweet spot generally represents striking a balance between two alternatives. On one hand, the earlier you take the first bird, the more time you will have for the second. On the other hand, the position of the sweet spot for the first bird may either facilitate or impede moving to the second bird as smoothly and rapidly as possible.

A pair that crosses one another poses two problems. First, they may present the optical illusion of changed speed/direction. Be aware of this possibility. Second, it is very easy to take your eye off the first target you plan to take when it crosses the other. Plan your shot so you can keep one target in clear view until you deliver.

Take your time. You certainly can't dawdle on doubles, but most of the time you do have plenty of time to take both.

Crossing Targets

A crossing bird crosses the shooting field at approximately a right angle or ninety degrees to the shooter (Figure 11.3). A bird crossing

Figure 11.3 A crossing bird. The bird emerges from a trap at the upper left-hand corner and crosses horizontally in front of the shooter.

at other angles is a quartering bird. Unless the shot is obstructed by natural barriers or the field has been taped/marked, the typical sweet spot for a crossing bird is toward the end of the middle or plateau phase. At this phase, the bird is typically level and the gun-hold position can be set to approximately the level at which the target will be taken. Occasionally, one must take a crossing bird when it is falling. In this case, adjust the gun-hold position and sweet spot so that the barrel tracks the bird not only laterally but down its descending path (Figure 11.2). Obviously, the reverse applies if you must take a crossing bird on the rise (see above).

The principal difficulty presented by crossers is that they require the most lead for a target of given speed and distance (see Figure 8.1). This is due simply to the geometry of the shot. As a general rule for establishing insertion point, insert the gun three or four inches behind the bird for targets at twenty yards or less. Insert the gun at the butt or center of the bird for targets over twenty yards.

One saving grace is that the shot stream is at its most favorable to the shooter on crossing birds. Think of a truck crossing in front of a passing train. The longer the truck, the more likely it will strike the train. Because of the variations in pattern in shot stream, modest overchoking is recommended on crossers.

Outgoing

Outgoers travel away from the shooter from a trap that is level with or below the shooter (Figure 11.4). These move away rapidly, putting distance between shooter and clay. Height, because of speed and distance, may be difficult to judge.

The shooter must pick up the bird by seeing around the barrel, if proper gun position is to be achieved. To do this, estimate sweet

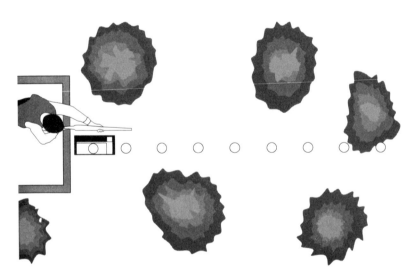

Figure 11.4 An outgoing bird. The bird emerges from a trap located just in front of the shooter and travels directly away from him.

spot, insertion point, and hold position. Pick up the target in your peripheral vision about six to eight feet from the trap by looking around the barrel. Hold your gaze at a point below the barrel and do not consciously see the barrel. When the bird is released and you first pick it up in your peripheral vision, begin your mount actively by pointing just under the sweet spot with your forearm hand. If the target is rising, the insertion point will be right behind the bird. Bring the gun up to the target, so that the target is covered by the barrel. Deliver then. As always, continue follow-through. If the target is falling, a slightly different strategy is necessary. Insert the gun in front of the bird, because the significant lead here is bottom lead. Specifically, insert on the nose of the bird or perhaps one or two inches in front of it. Focus on the bird, deliver, and follow through.

Doubles on outgoers may prove particularly difficult because the two clays may not behave similarly *at the time each shot is taken.* Analyze each target carefully and make sure that it does not change from a rising to a falling target while you are taking it. The second bird may convert from a rising to a falling bird while you take the first bird. Even more tricky is the situation when both birds are falling at taking, because the spring of the trap does not hurl the doubled weight as powerfully as a single.

Incomers

Incoming clays are designed to simulate driven birds such as grouse or pheasant and frequently come from a tower or platform (Figure 11.5). There are two basic types of incomers: birds that pass over the head of the shooter and birds that fall in front of the shooter (and are therefore dropping shots) (Figure 11.6).

The overhead passing shot is obviously subject to the problem of improper perception of height. In a typical shot, the sweet spot lies before the bird reaches the shooter. Hold the gun slightly in advance of the sweet spot and catch the target six to eight feet from the trap in your peripheral vision. As you bring the target into

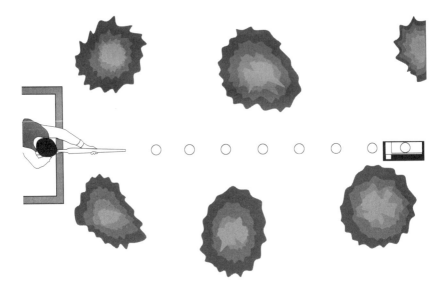

Figure 11.5 An incoming bird. The bird emerges from a trap located in front of the shooter and travels directly toward the shooter.

focus, insert the gun just behind the bird, pull through, deliver, and follow through the bird. Typically, you should deliver when you have covered the bird or pulled just ahead of it. You will usually lose sight of the bird for just a fraction of a second; when it re-appears, deliver.

Falling incomers pose different problems. The farther the bird has traveled from the apex, the faster it is falling. The least amount of lead is required when the bird has just started its fall; the most is required just before it hits the ground. The optimum place for taking the shot, viewed from this consideration only, is just when the bird breaks and begins to fall. This advantage must be balanced against the distance at which the break occurs.

Once the shooter has selected the point at which he proposes to take the bird, establish a visual pickup point to bring the bird into focus at the desired sweet spot. As the bird moves to this spot, insert the gun beneath the bird and deliver the shot when you

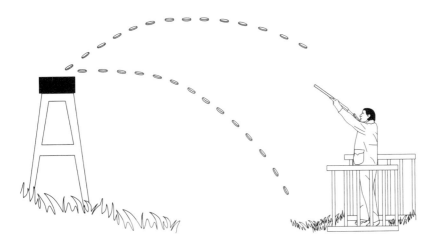

Figure 11.6 Two types of incoming birds. Incoming birds traveling directly to the shooter may die in front of the shooter or may pass over the shooter's head.

judge that sufficient lead has been established. You must program your computer in advance of taking the shot. It may take you a few shots on a particular bird to establish the requisite amount of lead. We recommend for birds taken right at the break point that you insert and deliver an inch or two in front of the bird. A bird twenty feet beneath the break point may require a lead of one to two feet.

Quartering Birds

Quartering birds are those birds that pass in front of the shooter in a ninety-degree arc extending from 7:30-10:30 at the left of the shooter and from 1:30-4:30 at the right of the shooter (Figure 11.7). Remember that outgoing quartering birds are gaining distance rapidly; take them as early as possible. The major difficulty presented by quartering birds is that lead is difficult to estimate. Specifically, *one tends to considerably overestimate* the necessary lead. As a generalization, deliver as soon as you cover the bird or just barely pull

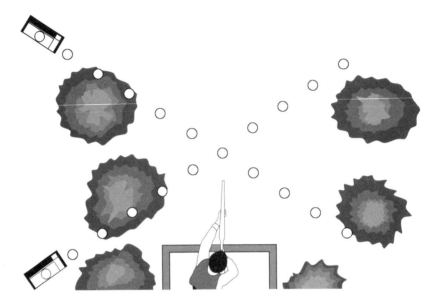

Figure 11.7 Quartering birds. In this picture, birds emerge from two traps at the right of the shooter at angles to the shooter's stand. The bird from the trap at the lower left-hand corner, is an outgoing quartering bird; the one from the trap at the left-hand top is an incoming quartering bird.

through it. With quartering birds, lead does not significantly increase with distance — over the range of twenty to forty yards. The visual perception of the appropriate point to deliver is the same for a close, quartering bird as for a far bird. This may be due to the fact that the shot stream works to the advantage of the shooter on quartering birds.

In general, take the bird as close to the trap as reasonably possible, where distance is minimal and lead is easiest to judge. Quartering birds are particularly difficult when they are above or below the shooter. The usual tendency to overestimate height of the bird is particularly in play here. One also has a stronger tendency to apply more forward lead than normal. Again, a minimum amount of forward lead is appropriate.

Quartering birds coming from behind the shooter are particularly susceptible to the optical illusion that they gain speed when they cross in front of the shooter.

Rising Birds

Rising birds, like falling birds, are characterized by the fact that the amount of lead necessary changes extremely rapidly (Figure 11.8). The best place to take a falling or rising bird is when the lead is changing at the slowest rate — when the bird is closest to the apex. We recommend taking these birds on the rise, where lead is more obvious and easier to control if possible. Optimally, one should take these birds just before they reach the apex. The bird at this stage has slowed considerably but is still under power of the trap and therefore still under control. The bird is easiest to see and

Figure 11.8 Rising teal. Rising teal have a rapid rise and fall.

read, and gun control is also easier. A falling bird of any type is very difficult, and a falling teal may not be a legal shot. Hold the gun approximately eight to ten feet short of the apex. Mount the gun directly onto the bird. The bird will disappear for a fraction of a second. Deliver the shot just when the bird becomes visible again behind the gun and continue the follow-through.

The major difficulty in rising birds is determining lead accurately. The rising bird leaves the trap at sixty mph but slows all along its flight path to a stop within seconds before it falls. Thus, these clays change speed and lead *very rapidly*. Take this into account and follow the bird no longer than absolutely necessary. A long follow-through of the bird (i.e., riding it) will suggest a lead appropriate for an earlier part of the path and therefore invariably will be too much.

The basic plan for rising doubles is to take one bird before the peak and, moving rapidly laterally to the second, take it at the peak. Which of a pair should the shooter take first? All in all, take the lower bird first. The paths of both birds and their relationship to one another must also be considered. If the two paths are parallel and directly vertical, take either bird first. If the two paths are parallel but slanted, take the lower bird first and then move to the other so the direction of gun movement for the first is maintained for the second, back-to-front.

Carefully analyze travel of the bird away from and toward you. Although not apparent from the butt, these clays may rise almost vertically, rise away from the shooter, or rise toward the shooter (Figure 11.9). The lead on birds moving toward or from the shooter will be somewhat less. More importantly, birds traveling away will need more choke. Remember, teal may be crossing/quartering as well.

When you set up, hold the gun higher — at least three quarters of the maximum height of the bird or fifteen or twenty feet below the peak. Pick up the first bird visually well below the hold point and immediately begin to mount the gun. As the bird comes out,

Figure 11.9 Types of teal. As in Figure 11.8, the shooter stands at the right. The teal may rise vertically toward the shooter or away from the shooter.

the left hand should start with it at that moment. Complete the mount vigorously by inserting the gun *directly onto the bird*; this point should be about five to ten feet from the peak. Actively pull the gun through the bird *without slowing*. As the gun comes on the target, don't stop the left hand; keep driving the left hand through the target. You will lose the clay for an instant. The bird will then appear under your barrel just as you deliver the shot. The bird should break a few feet above the insertion point or approximately ten feet below the peak. *Without observing the fate of the first bird*, move the gun laterally to the second bird; take it *at the peak* or just before. Shoot right at the second bird; cover it up and deliver with hardly any lead (*falling birds* are discussed under incoming).

Figure 11.10 A passing bird.

Passing Birds

A passing bird comes directly behind and over the head of the shooter (Figure 11.10). One key to taking a passing bird is not letting the barrel block vision of the bird. Look above you. Hold the gun slightly in advance of and below the sweet spot. When you call for the bird, pick up the blur or flash of the target in your peripheral vision. At exactly that moment begin your mount by pointing the forearm toward the target. Bring the gun toward but always *beneath the path of the bird* so that it is never obscured. Insert just behind and below the bird, and deliver when you pass through the bird.

The passing bird, like the rising teal, is one of two shots where the usual method we recommend must be modified. An overhead passing shot is falling, but deceptively so. Because the shooter is beneath the target, the amount of fall is frequently underestimated. This means more bottom lead is necessary than you might anticipate. Because the target is falling in front of you, pulling through the target will block your view of the target for a few seconds, producing an easy source for misses. You will also tend to deliver the shot when you pull through the target and thus shoot above or behind. The appropriate method for a passing target is to move the gun into but slightly beneath the path of the bird (Figure 11.11). That is, bring the gun barrel up into the bottom and the leading edge of the bird *so that the bird is always in view*. Pull through the bird rapidly; this will automatically give your instincts the right amount of lead to take the bird.

Special Applications of the Foregoing

The rabbit or skipper is basically a crossing or quartering bird beneath the shooter. Use the basic methods described above for quartering or crossing shots. The key point is not to overestimate the height of the target; your natural tendency will be to overshoot.

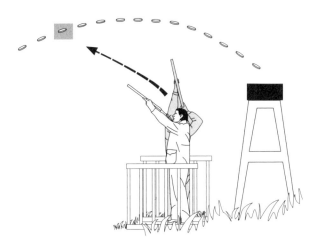

Figure 11.11 Insertion of the gun on a passing bird. Note that the gun never passes completely through the bird so as to block vision of the bird at any time.

Typically with the rabbit, the stand lies level with or even above the path where the rabbit will roll at a distance of twenty to forty yards. If the stand is elevated, this becomes greater. Thus, the angle of the gun from the shooter to the target is downward. As in all such shots, this distorts the shot pattern. Hold the barrel at the height of where you anticipate the clay will be taken. For almost all rabbits, shoot somewhat beneath the rabbit. For a rabbit of an intermediate distance (say twenty-five yards), begin by centering your gun two inches below the rabbit.

One of the challenges posed by the rabbit is the atomic or bouncing bunny. Actually, these are the easiest to take. When the bunny bounces, it is easier to take because its forward motion has been slowed. For bouncers, take the bunny on the rise, where chances of shooting over the target are reduced rather than at the peak or falling. A falling rabbit is liable to bounce a second time, so that you may shoot under it.

Fur and feather is one of the classic shots in sporting clays. The usual order is fur and then feather, though on some courses there will be a mixture; occasionally the fur will be the second shot.

In shooting at the rabbit, you scare the feather, which then flies (i.e., exits the trap). It generally tracks in the same direction as the rabbit, since most courses use only one trapper and one trap. When you deliver on the rabbit, don't watch your break. Immediately after delivery, begin to set up for the feather. To do so, you must get the gun back toward the trap. Be aggressive in getting back because you must outrun the trapper, and in this is situation the trapper can easily beat you. When you bring the gun back for the second target, don't bring it back too far because the bird will pass your barrel, resulting in a panic swing at many times the speed of the bird in order to catch up, and you will misjudge lead. If you are not set up when the feather is thrown, your timing will be out of sync with that of the clay. A crossing feather is easier than a quartering because you tend to shoot in front of a quartering bird. In most cases, don't remount the gun unless you have time to reestablish all your basics. Leave the gun mounted, move your eyes back to the trap, pick up the blur of the bird, insert, deliver, and follow through.

The *flush* is a variant of the overhead incomer where the bird is either very rapid, the distance between shooter and trap is short, or both. In this shot, time is the limiting factor. Flushes are also typically associated with demands on the shooter to reload as rapidly as possible. If time is the limiting factor, make your moves as aggressively as possible and hold closer to the trap. Pick up the bird as soon as you can. If you have not taken the bird before it reaches directly overhead, the chances of a miss are high.

In the *quail walk*, the shooter walks down a path or paths and is given birds to simulate quail at the discretion of the trapper. These birds may be of many types and can include passers, crossers, and quartering shots presented at the height of the shooter, above the

Figure 11.12 A quail walk.

shooter, or below. Determine the basic situation and take the bird according to the general principles outlined above.

Three additional key points need to be made. First, pick up the bird as quickly as you can in your peripheral vision and begin your mount as soon as you pick up the bird. Second, hold the gun in a way to minimize movement during the mount. If there is an overhead bird, do not hold the gun in the typical hunter's position across the body. Rather, hold the gun pointed in the anticipated direction of the target's flight and align the barrel below the master eye. You can rapidly raise the gun and mount it on a passing bird. Third, change your walk. If you walk normally and are presented a bird when your off leg is behind, you will have to take one or one and a half steps to come into shooting position. Walk somewhat like a crab. Extend the off leg forward. Pull up the other leg. Repeat. In this way, you are ready to take the bird at any time.

Swivels, crazy quail, and bird brains have one thing in common. In each, the target path is not known to the shooter until the target emerges. A shot from a swivel trap is probably the simplest form of this shot and typically presents targets in one of three or four directions (e.g., right quartering/crossing, straightaway/outgoing, or left quartering/crossing) at the choice of the trapper. Crazy quail may present birds in an arc of 340°. Bird brain, using a computer and up to eighty traps, is the most complex of these shots and can present targets, low or overhead, at any angle from 360° around the shooter.

For each, the basic principles are two. First, hold the gun centrally between the possible targets, so that any target is maximally accessible. Second, scan the entire target-presentation area rapidly and continuously with your peripheral vision. When you catch the first blur of the target, point your forefinger toward it, mount the gun, and deliver. This is instinctive shooting at its most challenging and best.

Rising teal are covered under rising birds.

Exercises:

1. Name the six basic types of shots in sporting clays and define each.
2. Name the three general modifying principles that can affect each of these shots.
3. Describe the problems posed in taking doubles.
4. Name the one key step in taking a crosser.
5. Describe how to take an outgoing shot.
6. Describe how to take the two basic types of incomers.
7. Name the most likely error in taking a quartering bird.
8. Review the key essentials for taking a rising bird.
9. What is the key difference between taking the other birds described here and taking a passing bird?

12

IMPROVING YOUR CLAYS GAME

Introduction

The first step in improving your game is to set definite goals for yourself. Monitor progress toward these periodically. Do not be rigid about this and do not be disappointed if you don't meet your goals perfectly. Set reasonable goals and move toward them at a reasonable rate. You are making progress when you are eliminating errors, even if you are not achieving the goals *per se*.

The key to improvement is regular practice. Begin by practicing at home. Practice mount and swing with two exercises. First, practice mount and swing in front of a mirror to which you have pasted a small dot as the target. Second, try mounting onto and along the crown molding separating wall from ceiling. Both of these exercises, if consistently used, will help you to mount and swing smoothly. A third form of exercise at home is mental. Simply reviewing a particular motion (such as mount) or a particular shot that bothers you will improve your muscular movements and help program your subconscious computer.

When you become proficient at clays, begin shooting on a number of courses. You cannot develop the broad game necessary to cover most contingencies on one course.

The most important element in improving your game is constant analysis. On the course, at the clubhouse, and at other times such as driving or at home, review the basics of your game and your shot-making/analysis capabilities. We have given you the tools to analyze these and to change them toward the ideal. By constant analysis, you will improve both.

Analyzing Your Basic Game

If you are having problems improving, analyze each step of your basic game (see Table 12.1). It is particularly important for you to analyze your eye position and movements, your hold point, your mount, your insertion point, your delivery point, and your follow-through. First of all, you must have mastered determining each of these points. Second, remember that errors do creep in, particularly when you make changes in any part of your style. All of the eye-hand-coordinated movements in your mount and swing are closely interrelated. A change in any of these or in anything affecting gun fit will modify other parts of your game. You must then go back through each part of your game, analyze each, and refine each. After making these changes, it will be necessary to go back yet again and fine-tune all the other elements of your game. Con-

TABLE 12.1 *Key Steps in Your Basic Game*

1. Do you hold beneath the master eye?
2. Does your gun fit well?
3. Is your stance correct?
4. Do you grasp the gun correctly?
5. Do you hold the gun correctly?
6. Do you pick up the target early?
7. Do you begin pointing then?
8. Do you insert at the correct time and behind the bird?
9. Do you bring the target to focus at the sweet spot?
10. Do you continue to follow through after delivery?

tinue to fine-tune until you bring all back into a harmonious balance.

How do you go about analyzing your basic game? First, replay your motions during a shot, particularly on shots where you missed. Second, view your mount in a mirror or on a home video. Third, ask a friend, particularly one familiar with your style and the methods we recommend in this book, to analyze your game. Lessons from a professional teacher of sporting clays are also an excellent investment.

Begin the process by reviewing the checklist given in Table 12. 1. In the clinics we give, it is striking how many people are shooting with a nondominant eye, an ill-fitting gun, or both. We believe that the most common source of error in one's basic game is probably failure to insert the gun until the clay is past the insertion spot or the target has crossed the barrel. Late insertion of the gun (*too long after the target has crossed the barrel*) means that you have to chase the target. This completely disrupts not only your integrated movements but also any rhythm/timing you have achieved in sync with the target.

The most common sources of missed birds in sporting clays and in wing shooting lie in move, mount, and shoot. Some of the most common errors are:

- You didn't look back and pick up the target soon enough.
- When you picked up the target, you didn't begin an active mount by pointing at the target with the forefinger of the forearm hand.
- You didn't insert the gun at the right point and had to catch up with the bird.
- You didn't deliver when your instincts told you to.
- You raised your head from the stock.
- You looked back at the gun barrel or, specifically, at the point between the gun barrel and the target to measure lead.
- You didn't follow through with swing.

- You weren't focused on the bird when you delivered.
- You didn't have the gun pointed at the bird when you delivered.
- You watched, on a double, the first target break and didn't move your hands, head, and eyes immediately to the second target.
- You tried to take doubles with one shot.
- You rode the clay too long.

When you can consistently eliminate these twelve deadly sins from your game, you'll be pleased with the results indeed.

Analyzing Your Shot-Making Capacities

Rate each shot you make, particularly those where you miss or do not break the target cleanly. Ask your computer: Where was my barrel when I delivered? For the best hits there is a feeling of purity that makes it very difficult to analyze where your gun barrel was. This is another way of saying that you did everything right.

Once you have determined where you missed a given shot, ask yourself why. First, is there a common pattern to your misses (right-to-left crossers, left-right hard-quartering birds, and the like)? Is there a flaw in your mount? Aside from problems with gun fit and master eye, a common problem is canting the gun barrel. This invariably causes the shooter to miss in a consistent way. If this is your problem, work on this aspect of your game and all the others until you have perfected a smooth mount where hand, eye, and gun come together smoothly at the right points.

The other possibility is that you're not seeing or reading the targets correctly. Review your analysis of each shot. Are you interpreting the true path, speed, angle, and distance of a target correctly? When you did not hit the target, did you carry out your plan correctly? Third, was the plan itself correct? Did alterations in your plan, suggested by analysis of misses, cause you to begin hitting the bird? By constantly checking these three factors, you should be able to isolate the element or elements in your analysis of the birds causing you to miss.

The best source for help in this regard is another shooter or a professional teacher. Ask your shooting partner, coach, or one of the better shots at your gun club how they read and interpret a given shot. They may not shoot according to this method but their insights as to the target's flight and whether it is dropping or not, its speed, etc. can be very useful. It is not useful to ask other shooters how much lead they see. Even shooters using the same method and analyzing the target the same way will see varying amounts of lead on a given target when they analyze where they delivered on a particular shot. What is important is to get from them how to read the target. Once you have done this and can see clearly where you are missing, continue to change your plan of attack until you have dialed in the shot correctly.

We strongly recommend regular practice. Ask yourself after every shot, whether a hit or a miss: How well did I take that clay? It is important for subsequent shots to modify your plan of attack if you were not completely satisfied with a shot. By critical and ongoing analysis, you can perfect your clay-shooting abilities.

Exercises:

1. Describe two ways of practicing mount at home. How often do you practice each of these?
2. Have you checked your dominant eye and corrected for this, if necessary?
3. Are you shooting with a good-fitting, well-balanced gun?
4. How many of the 12 deadly sins of low-gun shooting are you committing at least once a week?
5. Do you think that your analysis of shots is accurate when compared to the best shooters that you interact with?

13

IMPROVING YOUR WING SHOOTING

The methods presented in this book were developed on the sporting-clays courses in response to the rising popularity and the challenges posed by the sport. Remember that sporting clays originated to simulate hunting. Although many shots on courses today do not resemble true hunting shots, the fundamental principles of hunting and clay shooting remain similar. In both, you shoot with a low gun. In both, you must be prepared to take a target at an indefinite time. In both, the targets are offered in a variety of presentations.

One of the first ways of improving your wing shooting is to use the clay course to simulate wing shooting. For example, at the start of dove season, see if you can arrange with your local clays course to set up a number of simulated dove shots, or ask that you be allowed to practice a variety of shots that you devise yourself around their tower. Similar simulated hunting sessions could readily be devised for quail, pheasant, grouse, duck, etc. The second basic way to improve your wing shooting is to employ the principles described in this book. A rising quail going away from you is a classic example of a straightaway shot described in Chapter 11. Likewise, a long, slow crossing shot is a good simulation of a crossing pheasant. You have learned how to take these shots. *The basic principles of shooting and mounting as well as taking these particular shots apply to the field situation.* It may be argued that sporting clays does not closely resemble hunting because you use a stand and call for the clay. In hunting situations, there will indeed be differences. One often knows in the field, however, about where one will stand to take a given shot, about when the shot will come, and about where the bird will fly. For example, your dog locks on a covey of quail. You know that the quail are ahead of you. You have some idea as to the most likely directions that they will take. You can then raise your gun to the ready position beneath the master eye. Walk forward keeping your peripheral vision open and scanning for the covey rise. Thus, to some extent, you have anticipated the type and timing of the shot and how to set up for it.

Exercises:

1. Have you mastered the basic principles of low-gun shooting as described in this book?

2. Have you used your local clay course to simulate the types of game on which you are most interested in improving your wing shooting?

14

SAFETY AND ETIQUETTE

Safety

In all clay games — sporting clays, trap, and skeet — everyone is proud of the superb safety record. Perhaps the biggest difference between hunting and shooting sporting clays is that the clay targets are controlled. Take advantage of that to maximize safety. You don't need to have your gun loaded, except when you are in the stand. You don't need any more shells in the gun than the number of targets to be presented. Load your gun only in the stand. Make sure you come off of the stand with an unloaded gun. As a courtesy to your fellow shooters, keep your breach or action open so they will know that you haven't forgotten a shell. Don't take any chances when firing. There shouldn't be anyone on the shooting field, but always check. If the trap boy emerges from the house or somebody else wanders onto the field, unload your gun immediately and step from the stand. Lastly, keep your muzzle pointed downrange or into the ground. In the case of a misfire, point the gun downrange. Wait several seconds for a delayed fire. Holding the breach away from you, open the gun carefully. Remove the misfired/unfired shell. Check both barrels carefully for retained wads.

Obviously these rules for clays must be modified for wing shooting. Nevertheless, most of them are applicable to wing shooting. A major difference between clay sports and actual hunting is use of the safety. In hunting, use the safety consistently. Do not take the safety off until just before you deliver. By contrast, maximum safety at clay games depends on not using the safety. Use of the safety only can give you a false sense of security. Rather, make sure that your gun is unloaded at all times except when in the stand, that you never load more shells than needed for the number of targets presented upon one call, and that you never leave the stand with a loaded gun.

Take all possible steps to insure safety, whether in the field or on the clay course. Accept responsibility for the safety of others. Always ask yourself before beginning your mount: Can other shooters, hunters, dog handlers/trainers, spectators, or people who have wandered onto the field by mistake possibly be hit when you raise your gun and move it in any possible way toward the target? Unless you can answer no definitely, *don't mount.*

For your own safety, always use earplugs and safety glasses. Remember that a shotgun can produce forty to sixty decibels of noise above acceptable levels. You need ear protection to keep that blast in the normal range. Foam plugs can give up to thirty-five decibels of protection if properly used. Earmuffs can give even more if the seal around the ears is not interrupted by glasses. Chips of wood, wads, powder, shot, and fragments of targets can fly back. Everybody on the course should wear some form of safety glasses.

Shooter's glasses, in an appropriate color to bring out the clays against a variety of backgrounds and weather conditions, are a very worthwhile expenditure for the serious shooter. Orange, vermilion, or bronze lenses are good for orange targets in sunny conditions, while orange to yellow may be better in mist. Pickup of black targets may be improved by purple. Use prescription glasses if you need them. Use the palest or least-tinted glasses possible; your eye, like a camera lens, loses depth of focus as less light enters. Many prefer blue-blocking capacities in addition on orange or yellow lenses because the longer waves of blue light make focusing difficult.

Etiquette

Etiquette in sporting clays and wing shooting is aimed at promoting safety and a pleasant shoot. Keeping one's action open and observing the utmost in safety precautions is not only necessary but good manners as well. It is difficult for your fellow shooters to relate to you if they do not think you are a safe shooter.

Most courtesies on the course or field are matters of common sense. Don't let your conversation intrude upon the consciousness of the shooter; respect their need for silence when taking a shot. Be cognizant of the shooter's need to see the target and to maintain his/her appropriate body space. It is very difficult to concentrate when another shooter looms in your peripheral vision or hovers behind/around you. Lastly, carry your unbreached double-barrel with the stock over your back and the barrels over your chest to minimize banging the barrel of your gun upon those of others.

The balance between following official rules to the letter and appropriate conduct when shooting with friends is delicate. In tournaments, one must obviously go precisely by the rules. When shooting with friends, particularly new ones, we recommend that you shoot clearly within the major rules. For example, use a low rather than a premounted gun — even if it is your first attempt at clays. While your score in an informal shooting situation is not important, a new shooter who displays little regard for conventions of the game may not be as welcome the next time he steps on the course.

If you are an experienced shooter, make newcomers welcome and help them. They will appreciate a little advice on shooting better, *if it is accurate*. Too much help is confusing, and incorrect/vague help is actually harmful. Give them encouragement and explain that ninety-nine out of one hundred targets, unlike in skeet and trap, is the impossible dream.

Venturing into deep waters, we comment on attire. Sporting clays, at least as we personally partake, is an informal sport. The perception of clay shooters in Wellies, tweeds, waxed cottons, checked shirts, ties, and knickers — whether appealing or abhorrent — is not pertinent to clays as generally shot in this country. Sporting clays is a loose and gregarious game. We and most of those with whom we shoot wear a variety of clothing, including T-shirts, shorts, jeans, and tennis shoes. By all means, wear what you like and feel most comfortable in. On the other hand, the sight of a shooter in shorts without a shirt and wearing flip-flops does little to put the best foot of the sport forward. All in all, you won't go wrong by dressing like most of the rest of us do in comfortable, casual, old hunting/sports clothes.

Exercise:

1. Imagine that you are teaching safety to your fourteen-year-old son or daughter. What would you tell them so that you felt that you had covered all important aspects of safety?

BIBLIOGRAPHY

1. Atwill, Lionel. 1990. *Sporting Clays: An Orvis Guide*. New York: Atlantic Monthly Press.

2. Bidwell, John and Robbin Scott. 1990. *Move, Mount, and Shoot*. Wiltshire, England: The Crowood Press.

3. Bowlen, Bruce. 1985. *The Orvis Wing-Shooting Handbook*. New York: Lyons & Burford, Publishers.

4. Brister, Bob. 1974. *Shotgunning, The Art and the Science*. Piscataway, NJ: Winchester Press.

5. Lewis, Jack and Comus, Steve. 1991. *The Gun Digest Book of Sporting Clays*. Northbrook, Illinois: D.B.I. Books, Inc.

6. Martin, W.F. 1984. *An Insight to Sports Featuring Trap Shooting and Golf*. Seattle, Washington: SportsVision, Inc.

7. Meyer, Jerry. 1990. *The Sporting Clays Handbook*. New York: Lyons & Burford, Publishers.

8. Smith, A.J. 1987. *Sporting Clays*. Waseca, WI: Argus Books/Willow Creek Press.

9. Oberfell, G. G. and Thompson, C. E. 1960. *The Mysteries of Shotgun Patterns*, Stillwater: Oklahoma State University Press.

INDEX